ISBN 979-8-89632-492-8

ANATOMY OF BREAKOUT AND PULLBACK TRADING

KAUSHIK AKIWATKAR

CONTENTS

ACKNOWLEDGEMENT

Writing Anatomy of Breakout and Pullback Trading has been a journey shaped by the support, inspiration, and invaluable guidance of mentors, friends, family, and peers. This book represents years of learning, practice, and refinement, drawing from both time-honored trading strategies and contemporary insights into market dynamics. It is a culmination of shared knowledge and collective wisdom, and I am deeply grateful to those who have contributed directly and indirectly to this work.

A book like this is never solely the author's work. Many readers will recognize their own ideas within these pages—sometimes enhanced, sometimes not fully capturing their original essence. In a way, I feel like I have merely brought it together for many others. This book also reflects my deep gratitude to those who have influenced my thinking on trading and investing over the years, including those who have passionately disagreed with me.

My deepest gratitude goes to the legendary traders and market theorists whose groundbreaking work laid the foundation for much of our understanding of technical analysis today. Giants like Richard Wyckoff, Nicolas Darvas, Richard Dennis, William O' Neil, Mark Minirveni, and Mark Douglas have inspired not only the systems presented in this book but also my approach to the market. Their wisdom continues to resonate with traders worldwide, and this book is a humble attempt to honour their legacy by adapting their teachings for the modern trading landscape.

A special acknowledgement to Prashant Shah, Founder and CEO of Definedge Securities. Prashant's profound contributions to technical analysis, especially his work on Point & Figure charting, have greatly influenced the concepts discussed here. His structured approach to trading and his insights into market behaviour have provided a solid foundation for the technical frameworks explored in this book. Beyond his professional expertise, Prashant has been a guiding force in this writing journey—always just a call away for advice, encouragement, and clarity. His humility and dedication to his craft are qualities I admire deeply, and I am grateful to count him as both a mentor and a friend. The Point & Figure and Renko charts used throughout this book are from Definedge's Zone and TradePoint software, and all candlestick charts are sourced from TradingView.com.

To my wife, Sameera, this book owes its very existence. Without her steadfast support and encouragement, *Anatomy of Breakout and Pullback Trading* would have remained an idea, scattered in fragments. Her belief that now was the right time to document my experiences has been the backbone of this endeavour. Beyond inspiration, she played an active role in shaping the book. This work is as much hers as it is mine, and I am deeply grateful for her unwavering presence.

To my mentors, colleagues, and my students who have influenced my journey, thank you. Your willingness to share insights, challenge my views, and push the boundaries of my understanding has been invaluable. The collective knowledge of market practitioners and educators is what keeps the trading world vibrant, and I am privileged to be part of this community where knowledge is freely exchanged, and growth is a shared goal. Special thanks to Rohith Jain, my team member, from *The Noiseless Trader* and Saahil Poojara for their invaluable help and sharing thoughtful inputs.

To my family and in-laws, who have supported me unconditionally throughout this journey, thank you. Trading can be a consuming pursuit, and your patience and understanding have provided the stability I needed to fully immerse myself in this work.

And finally, to my readers—thank you for choosing this book. I am honoured to share these insights with you. I hope Anatomy of Breakout and Pullback Trading not only serves as a guide to trading systems but also inspires you to continuously learn, refine, and grow. Trading is a journey of both skill and personal growth, and I am grateful to be part of yours.

To everyone who has been a part of this journey—your contributions are what make this book. Anything of value that you take from these pages is a credit to them.

Thank you.

PREFACE

Welcome to Anatomy of Breakout and Pullback Trading, a comprehensive journey into both foundational and advanced aspects of technical analysis in trading. Breakouts and pullbacks serve as the cornerstone of many trading systems, forming the basis for strategies that traders have relied upon for over a century. Historically, these strategies were manually tracked by veteran traders who pioneered classical trading theories. With this book, I aim to bridge the timeless wisdom of these early strategies with the modern tools and techniques that can enhance their relevance and effectiveness in today's market.

The concepts you will find here are presented the way I have come to understand them through years of consistent practice. Everything I share is borrowed, in one way or another, from veteran traders and brilliant minds in the field of trading. My understanding is built on the foundations they laid, and credit for anything you learn from this book goes entirely to them.

Markets have been traded for over a century, and in the year 2024, I offer this book as an honest attempt to contribute to the body of knowledge on trading and investing. You may find some of my insights and methods familiar or similar to those of other market practitioners, as certain principles are universally acknowledged among successful traders. I hope you consider this book a sincere effort to educate and foster the thought processes essential for long-term success in trading and investing.

Throughout this book, you will find a blend of classical strategies and nuanced adaptations. Most of the systems discussed here, such as the Darvas Box, Turtle Trading, and other breakout strategies, originated in the early 1900s or even before the computer era, when sophisticated software was non-existent. Recognizing the advancements in technology, I have taken the liberty to modify these setups where I felt doing so would add or enhance the edge of the system. For example, while Mark Minervini uses Simple Moving Averages (SMA) in his analysis, I have opted for Exponential Moving Averages (EMA) to reflect a more immediate reaction to price movements. These minor adjustments aim to make these classic strategies even more effective in today's rapidly evolving market landscape.

This book serves as a structured guide for traders who wish to master breakout and pullback trading. By compiling and simplifying classical theories, I provide clear guidelines for entries, exits, stop-loss strategies, and ideal timeframes. Each concept is supported by multiple case studies to aid practical understanding, ensuring that you not only grasp the theory but also see how it unfolds in real market conditions. Additionally, I have dedicated sections to fundamental analysis, demonstrating how to incorporate it effectively to identify fundamentally strong stocks that align well with technical setups.

In my experience, many traders spend years in the market without seeing the profitability they desire. This book is crafted with them in mind—a step-by-step guide to help uncover what might be missing from their current approach. The chapters offer an in-depth analysis of various trading techniques, aiming to connect these concepts with the psychological resilience required to succeed in the financial markets. You will find a dedicated focus on trading psychology, as mastering the mind is as critical as mastering any strategy.

Beyond technical setups, I share insights from my own journey, along with lessons drawn from icons outside the trading world who embody the qualities essential for success. Figures like Mahendra Singh Dhoni,

Lata Mangeshkar, Sachin Tendulkar, and Shah Rukh Khan exemplify traits such as calmness, precision, adaptability, and resilience—qualities that traders, too, must cultivate. These stories, woven into the technical teachings, bring a human element to the book, reminding us that success in trading, as in life, is shaped by who we are as much as by what we do.

This book will guide you in building a holistic trading framework. You will learn not only how to identify optimal trade setups but also how to protect your capital and manage risk effectively. With chapters dedicated to position sizing, trailing stop-loss methods, and risk management, the aim is to help you develop a sustainable trading practice that aligns with your personal goals. Each position-sizing technique—be it a fixed percentage risk, ATR-based approach, or the Kelly Criterion—will provide you with practical tools to balance risk and reward in a way that suits your trading style.

I have written Anatomy of Breakout and Pullback Trading not merely as a manual but as a guide for building a sustainable trading career. My hope is that this book becomes a reliable companion in your journey, helping you cultivate both the technical skills and the mindset necessary for long-term success in the markets. Thank you for joining me on this journey—I am excited to share the strategies, insights, and lessons I have gathered over the years, and I hope this book will serve as a valuable resource as you pursue profitability and mastery in trading.

Kaushik Akiwatkar

Chapter 1

TREND ANALYSIS

. . . .

When I first delved into the world of trading, one of the most common mistakes I encountered—and one that many traders continue to make—is incorrect stock selection. Most traders have gone through the frustration of selecting a stock that appeared to have potential, only to witness its further decline. This scenario is often referred to by the famous adage, "catching a falling knife." In the financial markets, this expression is used to describe the situation where an investor buys a stock after a significant drop in its price, hoping it will rebound, only to see it continue to tumble, often leaving a substantial dent in their portfolio.

But how can we avoid such pitfalls? The answer lies in a fundamental aspect of technical analysis: trend analysis. Understanding and correctly identifying trends can help you pick the right stock at the right time, helping you avoid the dreaded "falling knife" scenario.

What is a trend?

A trend represents the general direction in which a stock or the broader market is moving. It is a pattern of change over time, and these changes can either be upward, downward, or sideways. Trends are not confined to the financial markets; they exist in all areas of life, including business, fashion, and even pop culture. For example, in the business world, a trend might be a gradual increase in sales over several months, signalling growth. In fashion, a trend might be a shift in clothing styles, and on social media, a trend is defined by what is generating buzz amongst the online community.

Trends are continuously evolving, and in financial markets, they are the foundation upon which traders base their strategies. By identifying trends early, traders can position themselves to capitalize on future price movements.

How Do Trends Work?

Trends operate across all industries, often starting small before gaining momentum. In the stock market, trends are identified by analyzing historical price data. For example, business trends refer to gradual changes in revenues or costs, while fashion trends highlight styles that gain popularity over time. Similarly, market trends indicate the direction in which financial markets move—whether upward, downward, or sideways.

Knowing the trends in the stock market helps traders make informed choices and go with the market's prevailing sentiment. When a trend is strong and confirmed, it signals a higher probability of success when trading in its direction. Therefore, the popular adage, "the trend is your friend," rings true for traders.

Trend analysis involves methodically examining historical price data to uncover patterns and tendencies that can help predict future price movements. In trading, understanding and identifying trends is essential because it allows you to trade with the market rather than against it. When you trade in the direction of the trend, you maximize your chances of success and minimize the risk of false signals—those pesky whipsaws that can erode your profits.

Traders can identify trends using various technical analysis tools, but one of the most reliable methods is through the use of moving averages. Moving averages helps smooth out price data, making it easier to see the direction of the trend. They are particularly useful because they provide visual confirmation of a trend's existence, helping traders make informed decisions about when to enter or exit a trade.

Types of Trend Analysis

When analyzing market trends, it is essential to categorize them based on two primary factors: direction and timeframe. Each of these factors plays a crucial role in how you interpret price movements, identify opportunities, and manage risk. Let us dive deeper into the two classifications.

Based on Direction

Trend analysis can be broadly categorized into three types based on the direction of the price movement: uptrend, downtrend, and sideways trend. You need to understand these trends to align your trades with the market sentiment.

1. Uptrend:

A series of higher-highs and higher-lows characterizes an uptrend, indicating that the market is steadily moving upward. This is often referred to as a "bull market." The market is in an uptrend when buyers dominate the market, pushing prices higher.

- **Higher Highs**: Each subsequent peak in the price is higher than the previous peak, signalling strength in buying pressure.
- **Higher Lows**: Each pullback or retracement is higher than the previous low, confirming that sellers are unable to push prices down significantly before buyers step in again.

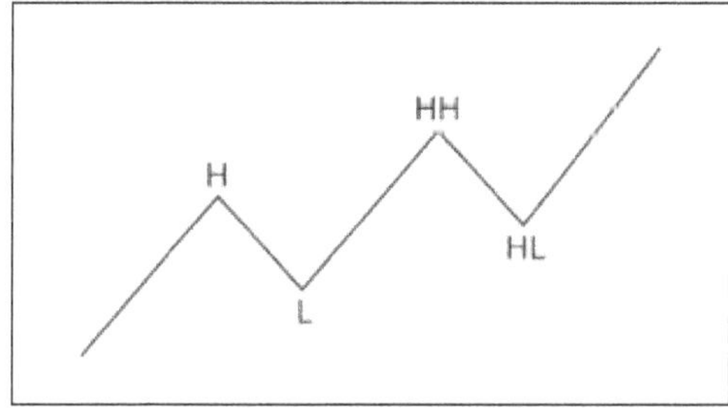

Figure 1.1: Image of bullish swing

Traders in an uptrend typically seek buying opportunities, entering long positions in the direction of the dominant trend. One common strategy is to buy on pullbacks or retracements to key levels, such as moving averages or support zones, expecting the uptrend will resume.

2. Downtrend:

A downtrend is characterized by a series of lower-highs and lower-lows, indicating that the market is consistently moving downward. A downtrend occurs when sellers are in control, causing prices to fall. When the price drops over 20% from its peak, it is called a "bear market."

- **Lower Highs**: Each rally or peak is lower than the previous one, signalling weak buying pressure.
- **Lower Lows**: Each subsequent decline takes prices to new lows, indicating increasing selling pressure.

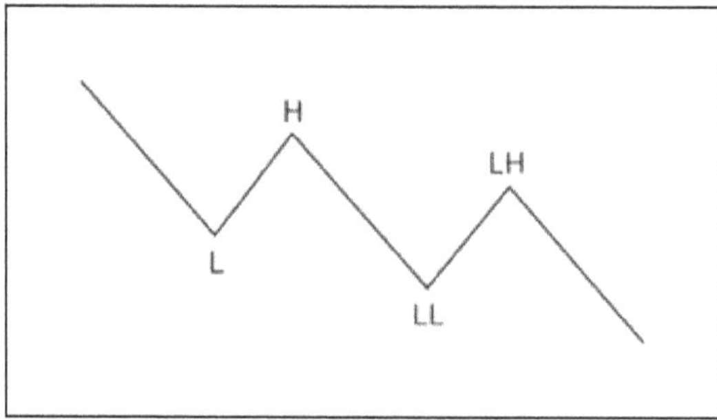

Figure 1.2: Image of bearish swing

Traders in a downtrend seek shorting opportunities, entering short positions to profit from the falling prices. Like in an uptrend, traders often enter positions after a brief retracement to a resistance level or moving average before the next leg down.

3. Sideways (Horizontal) Trend:

A sideways trend happens when the price stays within a horizontal range, without enough strength from buyers or sellers to move the market in a specific direction. In this phase, the price fluctuates between support and resistance levels without a clear upward or downward trajectory.

- **Range-Bound Movements**: Prices typically oscillate between a horizontal support level (where buyers enter the market) and a horizontal resistance level (where sellers dominate).
- **No Clear Direction**: Unlike uptrends or downtrends, sideways markets lack strong momentum, making it difficult for traders to profit from directional moves.

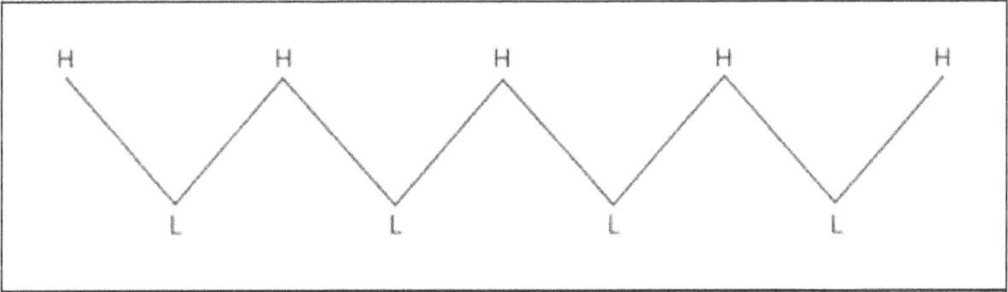

Figure 1.3: Image of sideways movement

Sideways trends can be tricky for traders. Numerous strategies that work well in trending markets, such as trend-following or moving average crossovers, may give false signals in a sideways market. Instead, traders often shift to range-trading strategies, buying at the support level and selling at the resistance level, or waiting for a breakout above or below the range to indicate the start of a new trend.

Based on Timeframe

Trend analysis can also be classified based on the timeframe over which the trends occur. Traders have different timeframes and focus on different trends based on their trading style.

1. Short-Term Trend:

A short-term trend refers to price movements that occur over a brief period, typically measured in minutes, hours, or days. This type of trend analysis is favoured by day traders and scalpers, who capitalize on short-term price fluctuations.

- **Short-term traders** focus on price movements within daily, 4-hour, or hourly charts. Their trading strategy involves quick decision-making based on market sentiment and short-term patterns.
- **High-frequency** trading systems or momentum-based strategies often rely on short-term trends, taking advantage of small price movements.

However, short-term trends can be more volatile and unpredictable, influenced by news events, economic data releases, and market sentiments. Traders must be quick and disciplined, as short-term trends can reverse rapidly.

2. Long-Term Trend:

A long-term trend refers to price movements that unfold over weeks, months, or even years. This type of trend analysis is favoured by swing traders, positional traders, and investors who seek to capitalize on broader market moves rather than short-term price fluctuations.

- **Long-term traders** typically analyze trends using weekly or monthly charts to identify broader market shifts, such as the start of bull or bear markets. They rely on these larger trends to make informed decisions about when to enter and exit positions, often holding onto trades for weeks or months.
- **Fundamental factors**, such as company earnings, economic indicators, and industry trends, play a larger role in long-term trend analysis, as these factors take time to manifest in stock prices.

Long-range trends are generally more reliable and less influenced by short-term ups and downs. Investors and traders in this category often ride these larger trends, capitalizing on the bigger market moves with less concern about short-term fluctuations.

Integrating Direction and Timeframe for Effective Trend Analysis

To effectively trade in any market, it is important to integrate both **direction** and **timeframe** in your trend analysis. An uptrend on a daily chart might look different when viewed on a weekly or hourly chart, so understanding how trends interact across multiple timeframes can provide deeper insights and improve trading outcomes.

For example:

- A short-term uptrend could be a temporary pullback within a long-term downtrend.
- A sideways trend on a long-term chart might indicate consolidation before a breakout into a new trend on a short-term chart.

Without considering both direction and timeframe, traders risk entering trades that contradict the broader market trends, leading to poor results. By mastering both aspects of trend analysis, you can make more informed decisions that align with your trading objectives and the current market environment.

Understanding Moving Averages

Moving averages are among the most fundamental tools in technical analysis, serving as a simple yet powerful method to smooth out price data and identify trends. There are two primary types of moving averages that traders commonly use: the Simple Moving Average (SMA) and the Exponential Moving Average (EMA). Each has its own special qualities, and it is important to understand these differences for successful trend analysis.

Simple Moving Average (SMA)

The Simple Moving Average (SMA) is calculated by taking the average of a stock's closing prices over a specified period. For example, a 10-

day SMA is the average of the closing prices over the last 10 days. The formula for the SMA is:

$$SMA = \frac{Sum\ of\ closing\ prices\ over\ a\ period}{Number\ of\ periods}$$

Although the SMA is easy to calculate and offers a clear average price over time, it gives equal weight to all data points, meaning each day's price has the same effect on the moving average. The SMA's lagging nature can be a limitation, especially in fast-paced markets that undergo rapid changes.

Exponential Moving Average (EMA)

Unlike the Simple Moving Average (SMA), the Exponential Moving Average (EMA) prioritizes recent prices, making it highly responsive to new information. The EMA uses a complex formula with a smoothing factor, giving more weight to recent prices in the moving average. The formula for the EMA is:

$$EMA = \left(\frac{Closing\ Price - Previous\ EMA}{Smoothing\ Factor} + Previous\ EMA \right)$$

We calculate the smoothing factor here.

$$Smoothing\ Factor = \frac{2}{Number\ of\ periods + 1}$$

For example, in a 10-day EMA, the smoothing factor would be:

$$Smoothing\ Factor = \frac{2}{10 + 1} = 0.1818$$

This means that the most recent prices have a greater influence on the EMA, making it more sensitive to current market conditions. The EMA's ability to react more quickly to price changes makes it particularly valuable for traders who need to respond swiftly to market movements.

In my trading and analysis, I give more weightage to the Exponential Moving Average (EMA). The EMA's responsiveness to price changes provides a more accurate reflection of the market's current momentum. This characteristic is especially important in volatile markets, where trends can change rapidly.

Therefore, whenever I refer to a "moving average" in this book, unless specified otherwise, you should assume I am referring to the EMA. Its ability to adapt quickly to new price information makes it my preferred tool for analyzing trends and making informed trading decisions.

Practical Application of Moving Averages

Moving averages, whether simple (SMA) or exponential (EMA), are versatile tools in technical analysis. They smooth out price data, making it easier to identify the underlying trend and helping you avoid the noise of short-term price fluctuations. Let us explore these applications in greater detail.

1. Trend Identification

One of the primary uses of moving averages is to identify the prevailing trend in the market. By plotting an EMA on a price chart, you can easily see whether the price is generally moving upward, downward, or sideways.

- Bullish Trend (Uptrend): When the EMA is sloping upwards, it indicates that the average price is increasing over the selected period. This suggests that the market is in an uptrend, and you might consider looking for buying opportunities. The upward slope shows that recent prices are higher than past prices, reflecting growing market strength.
- Bearish Trend (Downtrend): Conversely, when the EMA is sloping downwards, it signals that the average price is decreasing, suggesting a downtrend. In this scenario, you might look for selling opportunities or avoid long positions.

The downward slope indicates that the market is weakening, with recent prices lower than past prices.

- Sideways Trend (Consolidation): If the EMA is relatively flat, it indicates that the market is in a consolidation phase, with no clear direction. This can be a signal for you to wait for a breakout or to avoid making trades until a clearer trend emerges.

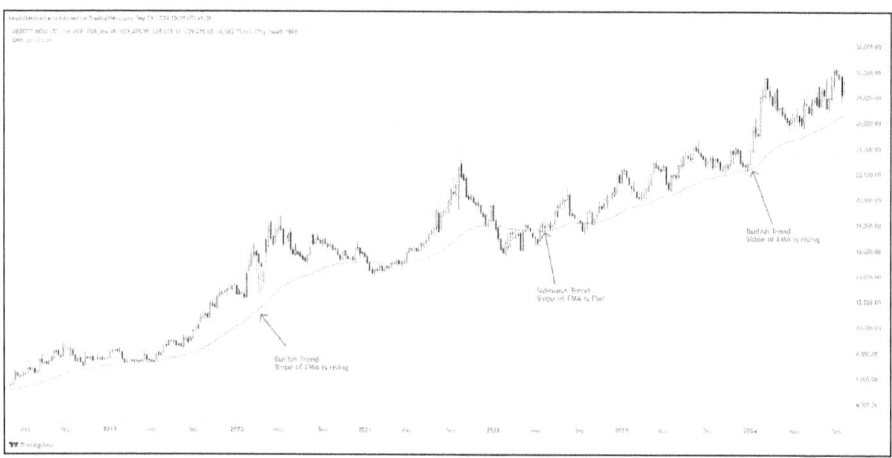

Figure 1.4: Weekly timeframe Candlestick chart of ABBOTINDIA along with 50-period EMA

2. Crossover Signals

Moving average crossovers are powerful signals used to confirm trend reversals or continuations. This method involves using two EMAs with different time periods—a shorter-period EMA (like a 21-day) and a longer-period EMA (like a 50-day).

- A bullish crossover happens when the shorter EMA line crosses above the longer EMA line. This crossover suggests that the recent prices are rising faster than the older prices, indicating the potential beginning of an uptrend. You may use this signal as an entry point for long positions. For example, if the 21-day EMA crosses above the 50-day EMA, it might indicate a good time to buy.

- A bearish crossover occurs when the shorter EMA crosses below the longer EMA. This signal suggests that recent prices are falling faster than older prices, indicating the potential start of a downtrend. You may use this as a signal to exit long positions or enter short positions. For instance, if the 21-day EMA crosses below the 50-day EMA, it might indicate a selling opportunity.

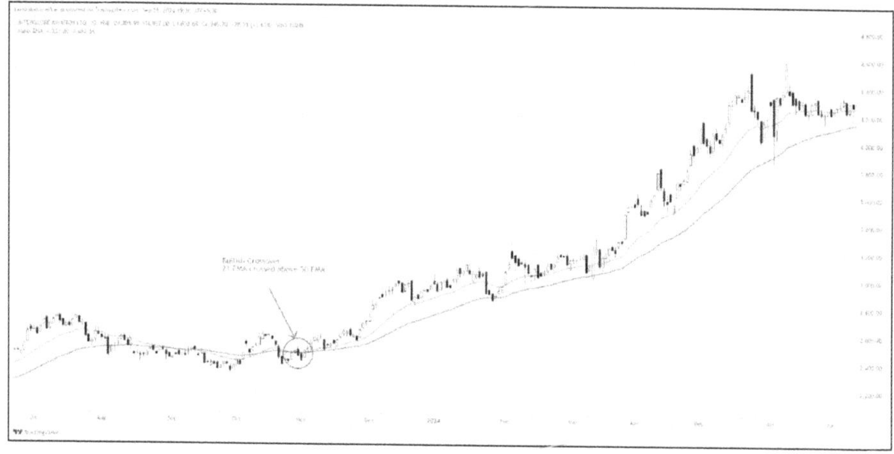

Figure 1.5: Daily timeframe Candlestick chart of INDIGO along with 21-period and 50-period EMA

As we progress through this book, we will emphasize specific EMA periods tailored to different strategies. To illustrate this concept, I have used the 21 and 50-period EMAs as examples. Bullish crossovers tend to carry more weight, given that most stocks and markets exhibit a natural bullish bias. Crossovers are particularly valuable because they help minimize the lag that comes with relying on a single moving average. By comparing the momentum of short-term price movements with longer-term trends, crossovers offer a more accurate signal for potential trend reversals.

3. Dynamic Support and Resistance

Another critical application of EMAs is their role as dynamic support and resistance levels. Unlike static support and resistance, which are fixed price levels, dynamic support and resistance levels move along with the price, providing a more flexible guide.

Dynamic Support: In an uptrend, the price often pulls back to the EMA before continuing higher. The EMA acts as a support level, where buying interest might re-enter the market. You can use this pullback to the EMA as a low-risk entry point, assuming the uptrend will continue. For instance, ITC takes a pull back to the 50-day EMA in an uptrend and then resumes upward. It can be seen as a buying opportunity.

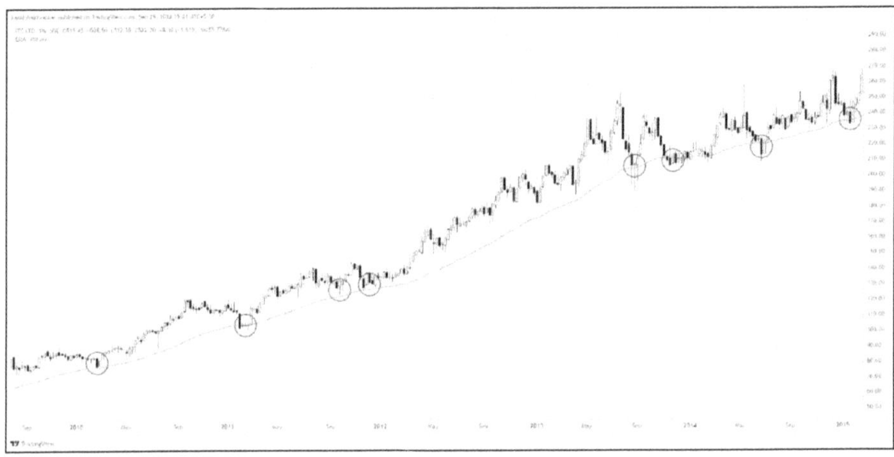

Figure 1.6: Weekly timeframe Candlestick chart of
ITC along with 21-period EMA

The chart of Dixon Technologies illustrates the application of dynamic support using a 40-period (40-brick in case of Renko) Exponential Moving Average (EMA) on Renko 1% Daily timeframe chart

In this uptrend, the 40-period EMA serves as a critical level, supporting price retracements and guiding you on potential entry points during pullbacks.

Throughout the chart, you can see multiple instances where the price pulls back towards the EMA (marked by circles). Each time the price touches or approaches the moving average, it bounces back upward, confirming the role of the EMA as dynamic support. This behaviour indicates that the market recognizes this level as a key zone for buying, preventing deeper price corrections.

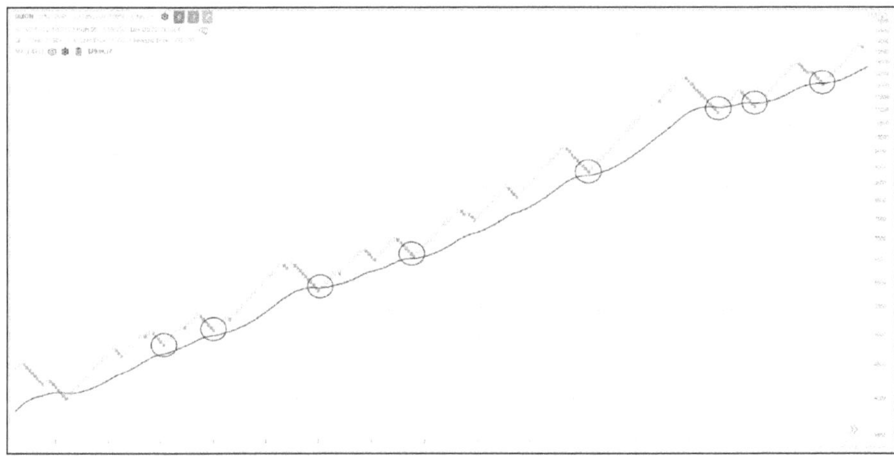

Figure 1.7: 1% Daily timeframe Renko chart of
DIXON along with 40-brick EMA

In Renko charts, where price movement is represented purely by bricks ('hollow' for rising prices and 'black' for falling prices), the EMA smoothens out noise and helps you focus on the underlying trend. The consistent upward slope of the EMA throughout the chart reflects a strong bullish trend. You could use these pullbacks to the EMA as an opportunity to enter long positions, aligning yourselves with the ongoing uptrend.

The relationship between the price and the EMA in this chart confirms the strength of the trend, offering clear potential entry points. You can set stop-loss orders to a technical pattern just below the EMA to minimize risk in case of a trend reversal. In this way, the dynamic support provided by the EMA helps ensure that you stay on the right side of the trend, taking advantage of pullbacks without being caught in deeper corrections.

The chart of Indian Hotels Company Ltd. (INDHOTEL) showcases the concept of dynamic support using the 20-period Exponential Moving Average (EMA). Throughout the visible price action, the price continually pulls back to the EMA, and each time it finds support around this level, it resumes its upward trajectory. This indicates that the EMA acts as a dynamic support level during an uptrend, providing potential entry points.

The black line on the chart represents the 20-period EMA. At each pullback, marked with circles, the price moves down toward the moving average but does not breach it significantly. Instead, it bounces off the EMA and continues the uptrend. This behaviour suggests that the EMA serves as a key area where buyers step in to support the price, preventing deeper corrections.

This dynamic support offers an opportunity to enter long positions when the price nears the EMA, as the trend remains intact. The slope of the EMA continues to point upwards, further confirming the strength of the bullish trend. Similar to the example of Dixon Technologies, the EMA helps avoid false breakouts and stay in line with the main trend while reducing risks.

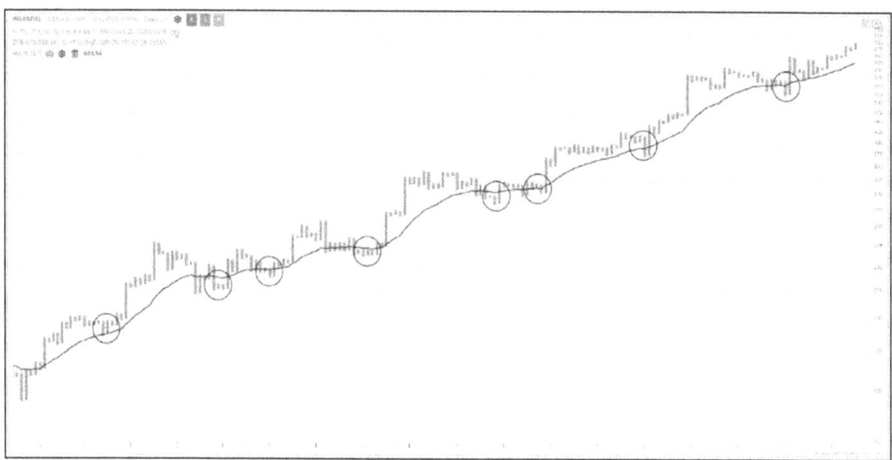

Figure 1.8: 0.5% Daily timeframe P&F chart of INDHOTEL along with 20-column EMA

By using dynamic support levels like the 20-period EMA, you can place the stop-loss orders just below the moving average, protecting you from potential reversals while giving the price enough room to fluctuate within the trend. This strategy helps in capitalizing on pullbacks without getting stopped out prematurely in the ongoing trend.

Dynamic Resistance: In a downtrend, the price may rally up to the EMA before resuming its downward move. Here, the EMA acts as a resistance level, where selling interest might re-enter the market. You can use this rally to the EMA as an opportunity to enter short positions, assuming the downtrend will continue. For instance, if the price rallies to the 40-box EMA on Renko chart in a downtrend and subsequently drops, it may be an opportune moment to sell.

The chart of Biocon demonstrates the concept of dynamic resistance using a 40-period Exponential Moving Average (EMA). Throughout the visible price action, the price repeatedly pulls back to the EMA but struggles to break above it, indicating that the EMA is acting as a dynamic resistance level during a downtrend.

In this case, each pullback towards the EMA (circled on the chart) shows how the price approaches the EMA line, only to reverse and continue its downward movement. This confirms that sellers step in near the EMA, creating resistance, which pushes the price lower. The consistent downward slope of the EMA further confirms the strength of the bearish trend.

The EMA acts as a critical level in determining whether the price has enough momentum to reverse or if it will continue in the existing trend. In this instance, each approach to the EMA is met with resistance, confirming that the downtrend remains intact. You can utilize such pullbacks as opportunities to enter short positions, placing stop-loss orders just above the EMA to manage risk effectively.

This example of Biocon illustrates how moving averages can serve as dynamic resistance in a downtrend, offering a visual cue to stay aligned with the trend while protecting against potential reversals.

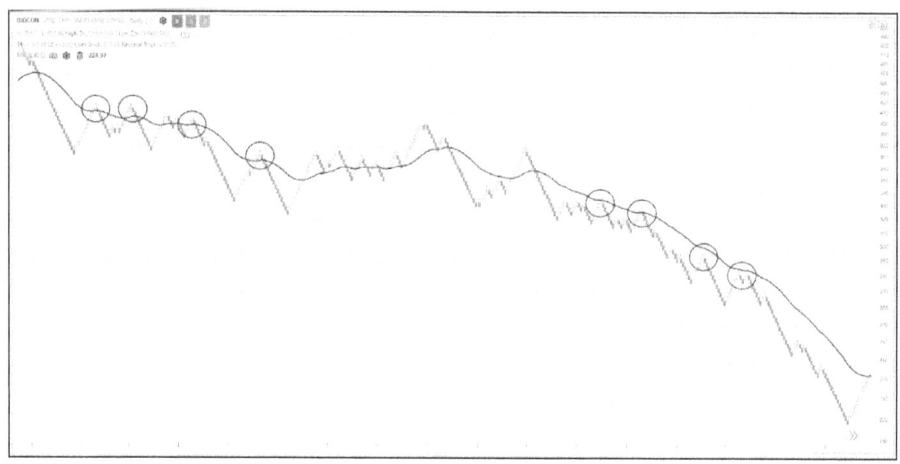

Figure 1.9: 1% Daily timeframe Renko chart of
BIOCON along with 40-brick EMA

This dynamic nature of EMAs makes them highly effective in trending markets, where prices tend to move in a series of waves. By identifying the levels at which these waves are expected to encounter support or resistance, you can optimize your entry and exit points, thus improving your overall trading performance.ce.

The Importance of Moving Averages in Trend Analysis

By understanding the nuances of SMAs and EMAs, you can tailor your trend analysis to fit your trading style and market conditions. While SMAs provide a smoother, broader view of market trends, EMAs offer a more responsive, up-to-date reflection of price changes. This responsiveness makes EMAs particularly valuable to capitalize on short- to medium-term trends.

As we progress through this book, the EMA will play a central role in many of the strategies we discuss. Its ability to adapt quickly to new price information provides a reliable foundation for analyzing and interpreting market trends, ensuring that you stay on the right side of the market's momentum.

To develop a successful trading strategy, it is important to grasp how moving averages are used practically. Whether you are using them to identify trends, confirm breakouts, or set dynamic support and resistance levels, moving averages offer invaluable insights that can guide your trading decisions.

Conclusion: Embracing the Trend

In the world of trading, understanding and identifying trends through tools like moving averages is essential. To increase your chances of success and reduce risk, trade in alignment with the current trend. Remember, the trend is indeed your friend, and mastering trend analysis is a crucial step in your journey to becoming a successful trader.

We are learning about trend analysis because, as we progress with this book, we will adopt and apply these concepts using moving averages in various strategies. Whether we are analyzing candlestick, Renko, or Point & Figure charts, the principles of trend analysis will be our guide. I will keep referring back to this chapter as we move forward, so it is crucial to grasp the importance of trends now, as this understanding will be foundational to everything we explore next.

By consistently applying trend analysis using moving averages, you can enhance your trading decisions, ensuring that you stay on the right side of the market's momentum. Whether you are a short-term trader or a long-term investor, understanding trends is key to navigating the markets with confidence. As we continue through the book, these concepts will become even more relevant, serving as the bedrock upon which we build more complex trading strategies.

Chapter 2

RELATIVE STRENGTH

In early 2021, I got introduced to the concept of relative strength, which I immediately found intriguing. Initially, I was skeptical, thinking that if we wait for a stock to outperform, we will miss a significant portion of the move from the bottom. However, my assumptions were soon proven wrong. After adopting relative strength into my trading strategy, I realized that when a stock outperforms, it often enters a period of strong momentum, where the price accelerates rapidly. I have witnessed stocks climb as much as 500% in a relatively short period—often just a few months—once they show relative strength.

The concept of relative strength has since become an integral part of my trading system. It is not just about spotting potential winners; when a stock begins outperforming, it often aligns perfectly with the classical trading setups and strategies, making it an invaluable tool for traders.

This chapter focuses on Relative Strength, a powerful tool to understand stock movements in the market and identify potential winners. Relative Strength will provide you with a systematic approach to compare a stock's performance against another stock or a benchmark Index, like the Nifty 50. This comparison highlights which stocks are outperforming or lagging, enabling more informed and strategic decisions. By integrating Relative Strength into your trading strategy, you can position yourself to capture high-momentum opportunities with enhanced returns.

What is Relative Strength?

At its core, relative strength is a method used to measure the performance of a stock or asset compared to another stock, sector, or market index. It helps identify whether a stock is outperforming or underperforming its peers, its sector, or the broader market. In technical analysis, analysts typically use the comparison of price movements in terms of percentage changes over a specified period to determine whether a stock is outperforming or underperforming its peers, its sector, or the broader market.

The basic idea is that two instruments' performance is compared to each other to check which of the two is performing better or worse. The instruments can be stock, sector, or indices.

Think of relative strength as a way to gauge a stock's performance in relation to its peers. Like comparing athletes in a race, relative strength determines which stock is winning in terms of price performance.

Why Relative Strength Matters in Trading?

For traders, relative strength is crucial because the goal is not just to make money, but to earn returns higher than the overall market. Identifying stocks with greater relative strength allows traders to target those that are expected to maintain their outperformance. This concept aligns with the famous quote from William J. O'Neil: *"What seems expensive and too high usually continues to go higher, and what seems cheap and too low usually continues to go lower."*

Relative strength is about focusing on strong-performing stocks and avoiding the ones that are falling behind.

What is Outperformance and Underperformance?

Outperformance occurs when a stock rises faster or falls slower than the overall market. For example, if the Nifty 50 index rises by 5% over six months, but a specific stock rises by 15% in the same time period, that stock is outperforming the market.

This example of BSE Ltd. illustrates strong outperformance as it gained 71.83% during the same time period when the Nifty 50 gained only 3.15%. This huge divergence shows strong outperformance by BSE Ltd., as shown in the chart.

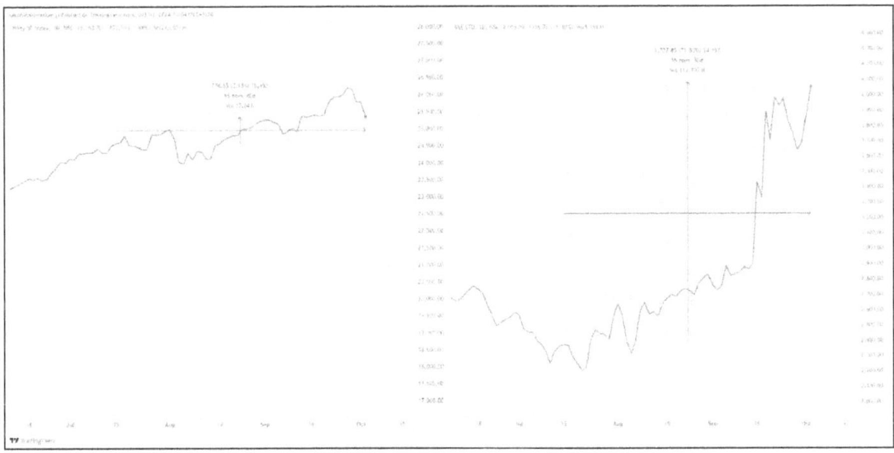

Figure 2.1: Daily timeframe Line chart of Nifty 50 and BSE

On the flip side, underperformance is when a stock or index falls behind the market. For instance, if Nifty 50 gained 5% over 6 months but a specific stock only rose by 1% or even declined in the same time period, market participants would consider that stock to be underperforming. Recognizing these distinctions is critical for traders and investors.

Understanding outperformance and underperformance is vital because these metrics help guide trading decisions. A stock that consistently outperforms the market signals strong momentum and may represent a solid buying opportunity. In contrast, an underperforming stock may indicate weakness, making it a candidate to avoid or sell.

Strength and Weakness

By employing relative strength analysis, we can identify which stocks are outperforming others and gain insights into their strengths and weaknesses in various market conditions. In this context, "strength" refers to a stock showing solid performance, while "relative" strength adds an important layer of comparison—it measures how that stock performs relative to its peers or the broader market. On the flip side, "weakness" refers to stocks that underperform the market or other stocks.

Figure 2.2: Image of Group-A

To better understand this concept, imagine two groups of athletes. In one group, the strongest athlete can lift 100 kg, while in the second group, the strongest athlete can lift 200 kg. Within the first group, the athlete lifting 100 kg is considered relatively strong when compared to the other athletes. However, if you compare this athlete to those in the second group, he appears much weaker next to the athlete lifting 200 kg.

Figure 2.3: Image of Group-B

Similarly, in the stock market, a stock could show relative strength within its sector but still underperform when compared to stocks in other sectors. The comparison in this analysis is why relative strength is so useful for finding promising stocks. It allows traders to not only see which stocks are performing well but also how well they are performing in relation to the broader market and other sectors.

How to Calculate and Use Relative Strength

We calculate relative strength using the following formula:

$$Relative\ Strength = \frac{Stock\ Price}{Benchmark\ Price}$$

By calculating the ratio of the stock price to a benchmark index like the Nifty 50, we can plot a ratio chart to visually assess the stock's performance relative to the market. When the ratio line is rising, the stock is outperforming. When it is falling, the stock is underperforming.

How is the Ratio Chart Plotted?

The Ratio Chart is the primary tool for visualizing relative strength. To plot a ratio chart, the price of a stock is divided by the price of the benchmark index or another stock. Then, this ratio is plotted over time, forming a line chart.

If the line on the ratio chart goes up, it means the stock is doing better than the benchmark. If the line goes down, it means the stock is not performing.

To enhance the accuracy of identifying outperformance and underperformance, we can add moving averages—specifically the 30-period and 60-period exponential moving averages (EMA)—to the ratio chart. Here's how it works:

- **Outperformance:** If the 30 EMA is trading above the 60 EMA on the ratio chart, the stock is considered to be outperforming the market.
- **Underperformance:** If the 30 EMA is trading below the 60 EMA, the stock is underperforming the market.

This methodology of using moving averages on ratio charts adds an additional layer of confirmation, ensuring that we are trading in the direction of strength and avoiding weakness.

The Importance of Relative Strength in Trend Analysis

The concept of relative strength will be mentioned frequently as we progress through this book. Whether identifying market leaders or finding stocks poised for a breakout, relative strength provides the context needed to select stocks that are in alignment with broader market trends.

As the famous market veteran William O'Neil once said, *"Buying a stock without knowing when or why you should sell it is like buying a car with no brakes."* By focusing on relative strength, we are equipping ourselves with the tools to buy and sell with confidence, ensuring that we are aligned with the strongest trends in the market.

Case Study: Nifty PSU Bank

Between July 2022 and the start of 2024, Nifty PSU Bank displayed a significant period of outperformance relative to the broader Nifty 50 index. This outperformance is clearly visible in the Relative Strength (RS) chart, where the 30-period EMA crossed above the 60-period EMA in July 2022, indicating the start of outperformance.

During this period, Nifty PSU Bank moved from around 2500 to over 7000 on the price chart. This 180% rise was supported by both strong market sentiment and continuous breakouts in the stock price within the sector. Every pullback and consolidation phase during this uptrend was a buying opportunity, making it a prime case of relative strength driving the momentum-based trading opportunities.

In early 2024, the RS chart showed consolidation, with the 30 EMA flattening against the 60 EMA. During this phase, Nifty PSU Bank began to lose steam, as reflected in the price consolidation at the 7200 level. This was a signal that outperformance was slowing down, and traders should start being cautious. Finally, by mid-2024, the 30 EMA crossed below the 60 EMA, marking the beginning of underperformance. The price of Nifty PSU Bank also started falling, confirming that the stock was losing strength relative to the market.

In this scenario, traders who relied on relative strength could capture most of the upward momentum and were alerted to exit positions as soon as the stock began to underperform, helping them maximize gains and protect profits.

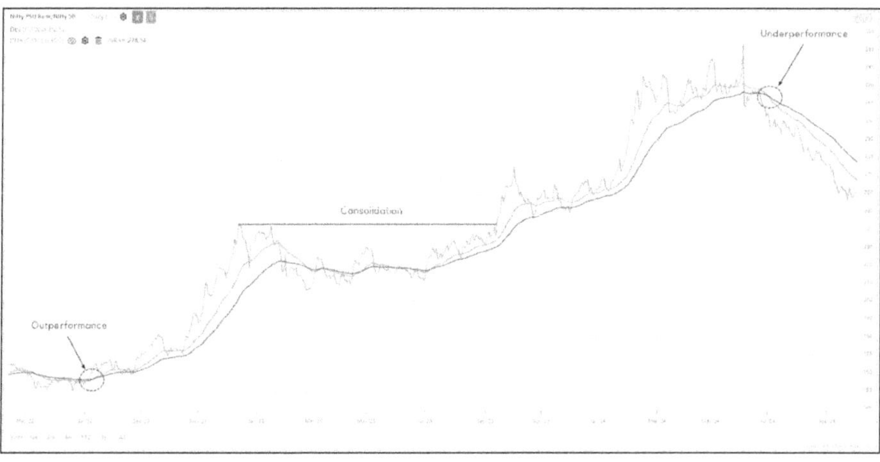

Figure 2.4: Daily timeframe Ratio chart of Nifty PSU/Nifty 50 along with 30 and 60-period EMA

Case Study: Nifty Pharma

The Nifty Pharma sector has exhibited several phases of outperformance and underperformance against the Nifty 50 index. By studying the ratio chart, we can observe how these shifts in relative strength played out over time. Starting in November 2020, Nifty Pharma entered a phase of outperformance, which was indicated by the 30 EMA crossing above the 60 EMA on the ratio chart. During this period, the sector gained momentum relative to the Nifty 50, and this trend continued until November 2021. This timeframe marked a strong uptrend for pharma stocks, largely fueled by favorable market sentiment towards healthcare during the COVID-19 pandemic.

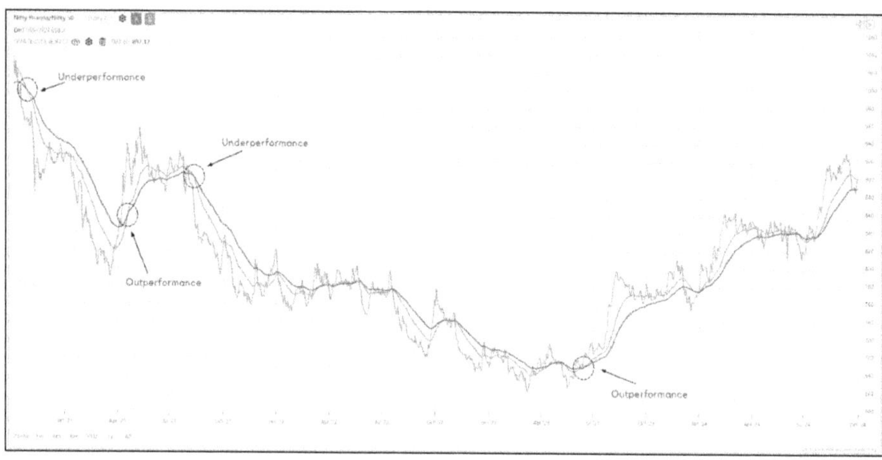

Figure 2.5: Daily timeframe Ratio chart of Nifty Pharma/Nifty 50 along with 30 and 60-period EMA

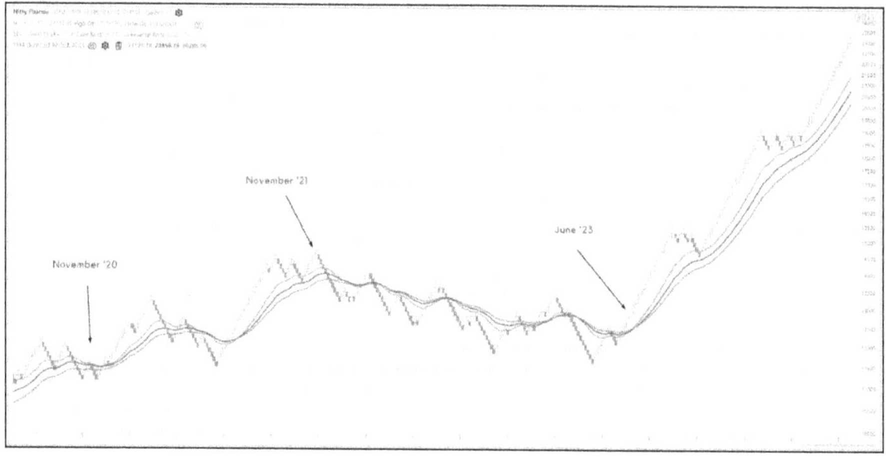

Figure 2.6: Daily timeframe Renko RS chart of Nifty Pharma/Nifty 50 along with 20, 30, and 40-brick EMA

Between November 2021 and June 2023, Nifty Pharma went through a period of underperformance. The 30 EMA crossed below the 60 EMA, signaling that the sector was lagging behind Nifty 50. Traders who were closely watching these signals likely avoided long positions in pharma stocks during this time, as the sector lost its relative strength. However, in June 2023, Nifty Pharma began another phase of outperformance as the 30 EMA once again crossed above the 60 EMA. This resurgence in relative strength was reflected in the steady upward movement in the price chart, providing several opportunities for profitable breakout and pullback trades.

Throughout these phases, traders who used relative strength analysis were able to adjust their strategies accordingly. Traders could take advantage of the sector's strength by identifying high-probability opportunities during periods of outperformance. Conversely, when performance is not good, the signals indicate that traders should either decrease or exit long positions to avoid potential losses. This case study of Nifty Pharma illustrates the power of relative strength analysis in identifying key turning points in sector performance, enabling traders to maximize gains while minimizing risk.

Case Study: Rural Electrification Corporation Ltd

In December 2022, Rural Electrification Corporation Limited (RECLTD) began to outperform the broader market, with its 30-day Exponential Moving Average (EMA) crossing above the 60-day EMA on the ratio chart of RECLTD/Nifty 50. This crossover marked the start of a powerful uptrend, signaling the stock's relative strength. From a price of 116 in April 2022, RECLTD rallied to approximately 450 by April 2024, representing a gain of nearly 288%.

Throughout this period of outperformance, traders using relative strength as a key indicator would have capitalized on the stock's momentum. The ratio chart's consistent outperformance allowed for several breakout and pullback trades, which were highly profitable during the stock's strong bullish phase.

However, in April 2024, the stock began to underperform when the 30-day EMA crossed below the 60-day EMA, indicating a potential reversal. This EMA crossover served as a cue to exit long positions and lock in gains. The shift from outperformance to underperformance was a signal that the stock was losing momentum and was not a good candidate for further growth.

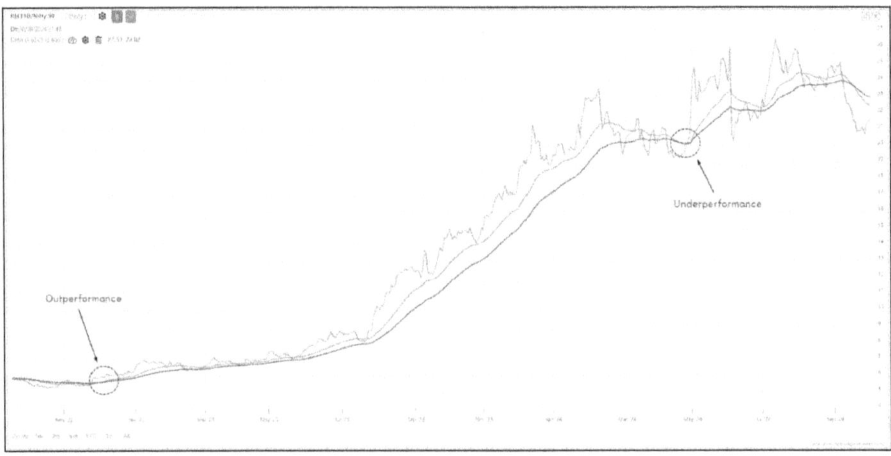

Figure 2.7: Daily timeframe Ratio chart of RECLTD/Nifty 50 along with 30 and 60-period EMA

Figure 2.8: Daily timeframe Candlestick chart of RECLTD along with 50, 150, and 200-period EMA

In summary, RECLTD's powerful outperformance period was a textbook example of how identifying relative strength can help traders enter and exit trades at opportune times, maximizing gains while minimizing risk.

A Foundation for Success

In conclusion, mastering the concept of relative strength is crucial for traders and investors aiming to identify stocks that are poised for significant moves. This chapter showed us that relative strength acts like a compass, pointing us towards stocks that perform well and steering us away from those that do not. This study helps us join the popular trends and also protects our capital by signaling when a stock is losing strength.

As we advance in this book, we will continue to explore how to apply relative strength across various trading systems. Whether you are using Minervini's SEPA and VCP methodology, the Turtle Trading system, or the Darvas Box strategy, relative strength can offer an added layer of confirmation for entries and exits. By aligning with stocks that show strong momentum and avoiding those that lag, relative strength becomes a powerful ally in maximizing gains and mitigating risks.

Going forward, we will build upon this base, using relative strength to enhance decision-making and consistently remain on the right side of the market. Understanding when to act on relative strength signals— whether it is to ride the wave of an outperforming stock or to exit when it underperforms—will give you an edge that sets your trading apart from the crowd.

Chapter 3

IDENTIFYING QUALITY STOCKS

In a book that focuses on technical analysis and classical trading strategies, incorporating a chapter on fundamental analysis is crucial for traders and investors aiming to identify quality stocks. While technical analysis helps pinpoint the timing of entry and exit points by studying price movements, the actual value of a stock is often derived from the underlying financial health of the company. This is where fundamental analysis becomes indispensable, as it provides insight into the company's long-term performance and stability through the analysis of financial statements, particularly the Profit and Loss (P&L) statement.

The P&L statement is a comprehensive summary of a company's revenues, costs, and expenses over a specific period. It offers a quick assessment of a company's profitability and operational efficiency, key factors that can influence a stock's future performance. Understanding the various components of the P&L statement allows traders to evaluate whether a company is fundamentally sound and worthy of investment, thereby complementing the signals generated by technical analysis.

As we progress through this book, we will delve further into how to participate in high-quality stocks using technical charts. The fundamental ratio filters discussed here serve as a protective mechanism, helping traders avoid stocks that are prone to "pump and dump" schemes or those belonging to questionable companies with weak fundamentals. By using these filters, we can focus on fundamentally solid companies with strong growth potential. When bullish patterns align with such fundamentally strong stocks, the opportunities they present tend to be highly rewarding, offering traders the lowest possible risk.

Understanding Key Components of P&L Statement

One of the key figures in the P&L statement is **Sales (Revenue)**. This represents the total income generated from the company's core business activities, often referred to as the "top line." Consistent sales growth is one of the most telling indicators of a company's overall health. Companies showing strong revenue growth, typically above 10% annually, often have the potential for long-term profitability, especially when supported by effective cost management.

Next, we have the **Cost of Goods Sold (COGS)**, which refers to the direct cost of producing the goods sold by the company. This includes the cost of materials and labor involved in production. Subtracting COGS from Sales helps calculate the **Gross Profit**, which reflects how efficiently a company can produce its goods. A high **Gross Profit Margin** (Gross Profit divided by Sales) is a positive indicator, suggesting the company has strong control over production costs and potentially a dominant market position. Companies with Gross Profit Margins above 40% are often considered having a competitive edge.

EBITDA, or operating profits, is an important measure of performance. It stands for Earnings Before Interest, Taxes, Depreciation, and Amortization. EBITDA helps gauge a company's profitability from its core operations before non-operational financial adjustments. A higher **EBITDA Margin** (EBITDA divided by Sales) indicates that the company is managing its operating costs efficiently. Margins above 20% typically show effective operational management.

EBIT is like EBITDA, but it considers depreciation and amortization expenses to show a company's earnings after maintaining assets. Like EBITDA, the EBIT Margin (EBIT divided by Sales) gives an insight into the company's effectiveness in managing operating and fixed costs, offering a clearer view of its long-term profitability.

At the bottom of the P&L statement is **Net Profit (Profit After Tax, or PAT)**. After deducting all expenses, including interest and taxes, this figure represents the total profit of the company. The **Net Profit Margin** (Net Profit divided by Sales) is a measure of how much profit a company makes for every unit of revenue. A consistently high Net Profit Margin, typically 10% or more, signals strong profitability and effective cost management. High-profit companies can choose to reinvest the profits, reduce debt, or distribute it as dividends to the shareholders.

Earnings Per Share (EPS) is an important metric for investors. It is calculated by dividing the company's net profit by the total outstanding shares. EPS is a reflection of the portion of the company's profit allocated to each share. Higher EPS values are viewed as indications of greater profitability. Investors frequently use this figure to compare the profitability of different companies.

While these metrics offer insights into a company's financial health, how do we determine the "ideal" numbers? There are no universally applicable standards, but some general benchmarks can be used to evaluate a company's quality:

- **Consistent revenue growth** of 10% or more annually is often a sign of business health and expansion.
- **Gross Profit Margins** above 40% suggest the company has strong pricing power or efficient production.
- **EBITDA Margins** of 20% or higher indicate efficient operational management.
- **Net Profit Margins** above 10% reflect solid profitability and good financial management.
- **High EPS growth rates** point to strong earnings potential and increasing shareholder value.

Besides understanding individual metrics, it is important to compare different companies using margins. Margins are calculated by dividing metrics like Gross Profit, EBITDA, or Net Profit by Sales. These ratios help analysts rationalize and normalize financial data, making it easier to compare companies of different sizes or in different industries. For instance, two companies with similar net profits might have significantly different Net Profit Margins, indicating varying levels of operational efficiency.

Types of P&L Statements

In addition to the core metrics, investors and analysts must comprehend various types of P&L statements.

- **Standalone P&L** reflects the financial performance of the parent company only, without including any of its subsidiaries. This offers a view of the company's independent operations.
- **Consolidated P&L** includes the financial results of the parent company, along with all of its subsidiaries. This provides a holistic view of the company's overall performance, including the profits and losses of its holdings.
- **Common-Sized P&L** presents each line item as a percentage of total sales, which helps in analyzing the relative size of costs and profits. This format is particularly useful for comparing companies of different sizes or for analyzing a company's performance over different periods.

Additional Financial Metrics

To fully evaluate a company's health, it is important to understand other key metrics beyond the P&L statement:

- **Market Capitalization (Market Cap)** is the value of a company determined by multiplying the current share price with the total number of shares outstanding. It gives an indication of the company's size and market value, with large market caps often signaling stability and smaller caps offering higher growth potential but with added risk.

- **Face Value** refers to the nominal value of a company's stock, set at the time of issuance. While it remains constant, it is used to calculate dividends and other financial ratios.
- **Book Value** is the net value of the company's assets after subtracting liabilities (Total Assets - Total Liabilities). It signifies the notional compensation that shareholders could receive in the event of a company liquidation.
- **Price-to-Earnings Ratio (P/E Ratio)** compares a company's stock price to its earnings per share. A lower P/E ratio may indicate undervaluation, while a higher P/E can reflect future growth potential or overvaluation.
- **Price-to-Book Ratio (P/B Ratio)** compares the company's stock price to its book value. A P/B ratio below 1 suggests that the stock may be undervalued relative to its assets, while a ratio above 1 suggests that the stock price exceeds the book value.

Traders can gain a deeper understanding of a company's performance by analyzing these metrics and their implications. To identify stocks with growth potential and financial stability, it is crucial to be able to read and analyze the P&L statement and other financial ratios.

Technical analysis aids in timing trades, while fundamental analysis helps identify valuable stocks. By assessing financial health through P&L statements and analyzing price behaviour using technical charts, traders can create a well-rounded strategy that balances timing with value identification. This combination strengthens the overall approach to trading.

My criteria to identify quality stocks

In my stock trading and investment strategy, I focus on participating in stocks that not only exhibit strong technical price action but also meet a set of fundamental financial conditions. The conditions I use help me identify quality stocks that are growing steadily by effectively managing their resources. The key financial criteria I use are:

1. **Current year's Return on Equity (ROE) is greater than the previous year's ROE:**
   ROE measures a company's profitability by revealing how much profit it generates with the money shareholders have invested. When the current ROE is higher than the ROE from a year ago, it shows that the company is improving its ability to generate profits using shareholder equity.

2. **Current year's Return on Capital Employed (ROCE) is greater than the previous year's ROCE:**
   ROCE evaluates a company's efficiency in generating profits from its total capital employed. A higher ROCE year-over-year indicates that the company is using its capital more effectively, improving its ability to generate returns on its investments.

3. **Net Profit CAGR of 3-Year above 20%:**
   This condition highlights companies that have consistently grown their net profits at a compounded rate of at least 20% over the last three years. Strong profit growth is a key indicator of a healthy, expanding business.

4. **Current year's Operating Profit Margin (OPM) is greater than the previous year's OPM:**
   OPM measures the efficiency of a company's core business operations. When this margin gets better compared to the previous year, it suggests that the company is either cutting costs or charging more for its products.

5. **Sales CAGR of 3-Year above 15%:**
   This condition ensures that the company has a steady sales growth trajectory, with a minimum of 15% growth per year over the past three years. Consistent sales growth is a sign of strong demand for the company's products or services.

6. **Yearly Sales Growth greater than 15%:**
   Besides the longer-term 3-year sales growth rate, I also look for companies that have grown their sales by more than 15% in the most recent year. This reflects the company's ability to maintain momentum and growth in the short term.

Conditions at a glance

Condition	Description
ROE > ROE 1Yr Back	Current Return on Equity (ROE) is greater than the previous year's ROE, indicating improved profitability.
ROCE > ROCE 1Yr Back	Current Return on Capital Employed (ROCE) is higher than the previous year's ROCE, showing better capital efficiency.
Net Profit (3yr-CAGR) > 20%	Net profit growth rate over the past three years is greater than 20%, highlighting consistent and strong profitability.
OPM > OPM 1Yr Back	Operating Profit Margin (OPM) is greater than last year, reflecting improved operational efficiency or pricing power.
Sales (3 yr-CAGR) > 15%	Sales growth over the past three years is greater than 15% annually, indicating steady growth in revenue.
Sales Growth Yearly > 15%	Annual sales growth in the most recent year is greater than 15%, showing short-term growth momentum.

When these fundamental conditions are met, they help me identify high-quality stocks that are fundamentally strong. From there, I analyze the price charts and technical patterns to time my entries and exits. This blend of fundamental strength and technical analysis ensures that I participate in stocks that not only show strong price momentum but are also backed by solid financial performance, increasing the probability of successful trades.

Case Study: ABB Limited - A Stock That Fits the Quality Criteria

ABB Limited is a textbook case of a company that qualifies as a quality stock, meeting the financial and technical parameters I have discussed. By blending fundamental analysis with technical chart patterns, we can assess why this stock was a great candidate for participation based on our trading strategy criteria.

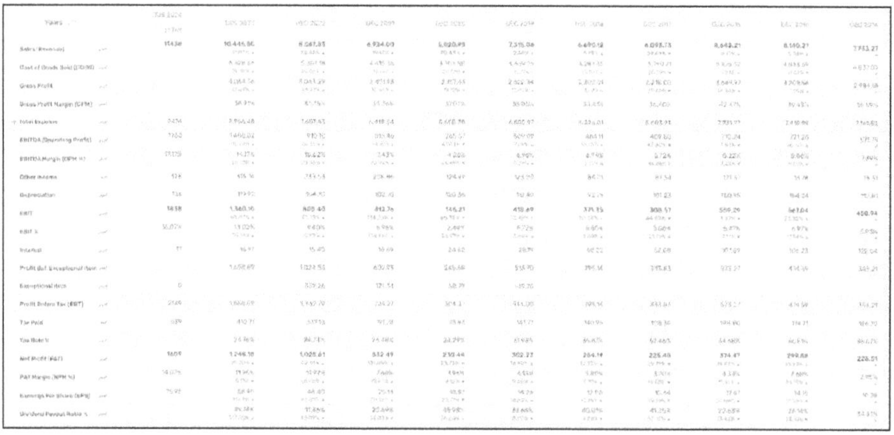

Years	TTM Jun 2024 (1 Yr)	[illegible]	[illegible]	[illegible]	[illegible]	[illegible]	[illegible]	[illegible]	[illegible]	[illegible]	[illegible]
Sales (Revenue)	[illegible]	10,445.86	8,067.85	6,934.00	6,020.93	7,315.06	6,490.12	6,098.73	8,663.21	8,560.27	7,753.27
Cost of Goods Sold (COGS)		[illegible]	5,351.98	4,455.16	[illegible]	[illegible]	4,281.35	5,740.21	[illegible]	4,855.04	4,837.00
Gross Profit		4,064.56	3,043.29	2,471.13	2,157.65	2,022.34	2,802.04	2,216.00	[illegible]	3,209.56	2,484.08
Gross Profit Margin (GPM)		58.97%	[illegible]	[illegible]	37.07%	35.00%	31.85%	36.40%	42.47%	39.43%	56.59%
Total Expenses	[illegible]	3,964.48	3,607.83	[illegible]	5,610.78	6,600.97	6,334.01	5,603.91	7,531.97	7,410.96	[illegible]
EBITDA (Operating Profit)	[illegible]	1,460.02	910.10	[illegible]	765.57	509.09	484.11	409.60	770.24	721.26	[illegible]
EBITDA Margin (OPM %)	17.17%	14.17%	10.62%	3.43%	[illegible]	6.90%	4.74%	5.72%	9.22%	9.86%	[illegible]
Other Income	[illegible]	415.36	243.58	203.46	124.47	[illegible]	86.21	87.54	171.61	54.99	76.51
Depreciation	[illegible]	199.92	94.90	102.10	100.56	50.40	92.14	101.23	110.95	94.04	[illegible]
EBIT	[illegible]	1,360.10	808.40	442.76	146.21	418.69	375.15	308.57	509.20	667.04	400.94
EBIT %	[illegible]	13.02%	9.60%	6.98%	2.44%	5.72%	6.60%	5.60%	5.87%	6.97%	5.05%
Interest	[illegible]	36.97	15.45	16.69	24.62	28.79	46.22	52.08	30.99	106.23	125.04
Profit Bef. Exceptional Item		1,658.69	1,022.51	630.23	245.68	535.70	395.16	343.83	923.27	434.96	349.29
Exceptional Item	[illegible]	0		339.26	121.51	58.79	-35.20				
Profit Before Tax (PBT)	[illegible]	1,664.69	1,342.70	724.27	304.1	544.00	399.56	343.63	578.27	434.59	354.29
Tax Paid	[illegible]	412.71	317.53	191.08	93.83	141.21	140.96	108.36	184.80	154.21	106.72
Tax Rate %		24.46%	24.71%	26.08%	24.29%	83.93%	46.63%	67.46%	34.98%	46.5%	46.67%
Net Profit (PAT)	[illegible]	1,246.38	1,025.61	532.49	230.44	302.23	264.14	225.48	374.47	299.88	220.51
PAT Margin (NPM %)	[illegible]	11.95%	10.92%	7.66%	3.94%	4.55%	5.80%	3.70%	4.32%	7.68%	2.95%
Earnings Per Share (EPS)	[illegible]	58.91	44.83	25.14	10.87	14.26	12.50	10.64	17.67	14.15	10.39
Dividend Payout Ratio %	[illegible]	24.38%	17.86%	25.64%	45.98%	83.66%	40.10%	41.25%	22.65%	22.56%	52.31%

Figure 3.1: **Figure 3.1:** P&L Statement of ABB from FY 2014 to FY 2024

Fundamental Strength of ABB Limited

The fundamental health of ABB Limited can be seen in its steady growth across key financial metrics. Between April 2021 and June 2024, ABB consistently met the financial benchmarks required to be considered a quality stock.

1. ABB consistently grew its sales, achieving a Sales CAGR of over 21% for both 1-year and 3-year periods. The increasing demand for ABB's products and services is reflected in the significant growth in sales.
2. The company's net profit has been growing at an impressive rate of 75.62% over the past 3 years, showing that ABB is effectively turning revenue growth into profitability. This significant growth in net profit is a strong indicator of financial health and solid operational management.
3. Operating Profit Margin (OPM) has seen a steady increase, reaching 17.17% in the trailing twelve months (TTM) as of June 2024. This growth reflects the company's efficient management of operations and production costs.

4. Return on Equity (ROE) has remained consistently strong, with an average of 22.94% over the past year, surpassing the industry average. This indicates that ABB is highly effective at generating profits from shareholders' equity.

5. The Return on Capital Employed (ROCE) averaged 30.79% over the past year, serving as a crucial metric in assessing capital efficiency. This further highlights the company's efficiency in generating returns on its invested capital.

6. The EBITDA margin for June 2024 was 17.17%, showing that ABB is good at making profits before considering financial and accounting adjustments. The growth of this margin over time reflects well-managed operations.

Technical Analysis of ABB Limited

ABB's price chart using Renko 1% Daily Timeframe from May 2021 to October 2024 consistently shows an upward trend, which is in line with the company's improving fundamentals. The stock price surged from approximately ₹3,997 in May 2021 to ₹8,110 by October 2024, reflecting a 106.79% price CAGR over the past year. This significant price increase correlates directly with the strong financial metrics observed during the same period.

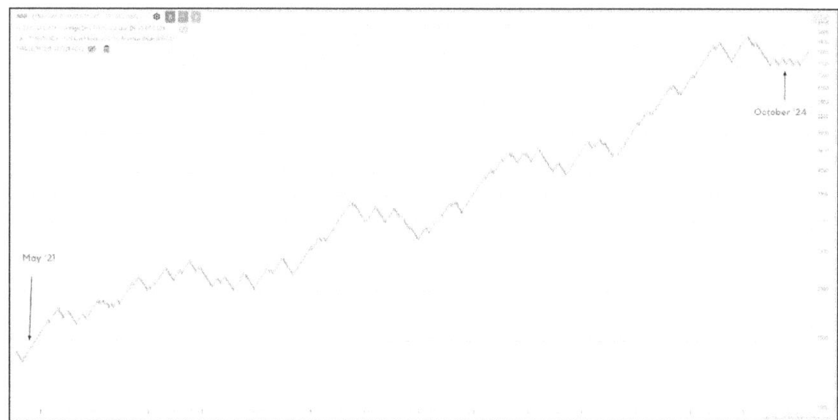

Figure 3.2: 1% Daily timeframe Renko chart of ABB

ABB Limited is considered a strong candidate based on fundamental and technical analysis. The company has shown consistent growth in key financial metrics, such as sales, net profit, ROE, and ROCE. Additionally, the stock price has shown a steady uptrend. This combination makes ABB a high-quality stock. Traders and investors seeking long-term growth and value should consider participating in this stock. By using fundamental filters and technical analysis, traders can identify stocks that are performing well in the market and are also fundamentally strong. This case study demonstrates the effectiveness of this approach.

Concluding Remarks

In this chapter, we have delved into the significance of incorporating both fundamental and technical analysis to identify high-quality stocks. These stocks not only exhibit strong price action, but also possess solid fundamentals. While technical analysis provides insights into market trends and optimal timing, it is the fundamental analysis, particularly the Profit and Loss (P&L) statement, that lays the foundation for assessing the intrinsic value and stability of a stock. By focusing on key financial metrics such as Return on Equity (ROE), Return on Capital Employed (ROCE), Operating Profit Margin (OPM), and consistent growth in sales and net profit, we can filter out stocks that are likely to generate sustainable returns. This approach allows us to avoid relying solely on price action and instead select companies with a strong foundation, thereby increasing our chances of long-term success.

As we progress through this book, we will delve deeper into utilizing technical charts to participate in these high-quality stocks. The fundamental ratio filters discussed here serve as a protective shield, helping us steer clear of stocks susceptible to "pump and dump" schemes or those associated with dubious companies lacking solid fundamentals. These filters ensure that our focus remains on companies that not only possess significant growth potential but also exhibit fundamental robustness. When a bullish pattern emerges in such stocks, it tends to be highly rewarding, presenting opportunities to participate with minimal risk.

The key takeaway from this chapter is that while technical price charts and classical trading strategies can inform us when to enter or exit a trade, fundamental analysis aids in understanding which stocks are worth trading or investing in. By combining both approaches, we can develop a more comprehensive investment strategy that mitigates risks and maximizes potential returns. By participating in stocks that meet the fundamental criteria we have discussed, traders can align themselves with companies that are not only experiencing growth but are also effectively managing their resources, thus ensuring a smoother and more profitable trading experience.

Chapter 4

CONSOLIDATION AND BUILDUPS

To kick off this chapter on Consolidation and Buildup, it is essential to recognize why understanding price behaviour during the consolidation phases is a powerful tool. Technical analysis is more than reading patterns—it is about interpreting market sentiment and decision-making through the lens of price movement. Consolidation is one of the most crucial phases in this process because it represents periods where the market is gathering strength before its next move. Whether your trading strategy focuses on short-term price movements or long-term trends, having a comprehensive grasp of consolidation can enhance your trade timing and minimize exposure to uncertain market conditions.

While price action during major trends can often be fast-paced and directional, periods of consolidation represent those quieter, sideways movements that allow both buyers and sellers to gather strength and recalibrate. In these phases, the market experiences a battle between bulls and bears, which can last anywhere from hours to weeks, or even months. During this time, price fluctuates within a defined range, forming a "buildup" of energy that often leads to a breakout.

This chapter guides you through the intricacies of consolidation and buildup patterns. We will explore the different consolidation patterns, such as triangles, rectangles, and cup-and-handle formations, as well as advanced methods for setting stop-losses for these patterns to manage risk effectively.

As we dive deeper into this chapter, keep in mind that consolidation is not just about identifying sideways price movement; it is about recognizing when the market is recharging and preparing for the next major trend. Understanding this concept can give you a substantial edge, as it offers clarity on when to stay out of the market and when to position yourself for potential breakouts with reduced risk.

Now, let us begin by breaking down the concept of consolidation and why it matters so much to traders.

What is Consolidation?

Consolidation, within the realm of technical analysis, refers to a phase where the price of an asset fluctuates within a well-defined range of support and resistance levels. During consolidation, the market appears indecisive as both buyers and sellers engage in a tug-of-war without either side gaining a definitive upper hand. This period of equilibrium results in sideways movement on the price chart, and it is often seen as the "calm before the storm," where price action stabilizes as the market prepares for its next significant move.

Consolidation represents a period of pause in the market. The forces of supply (sellers) and demand (buyers) evenly match, resulting in price fluctuations within a tight range. During this phase, volatility decreases, and the market "calms down," as traders expect the next major move. Depending on the asset or market, consolidation can last anywhere from a few hours to several months, making it a flexible pattern that occurs across different timeframes.

From a practical perspective, consolidation is a vital phase for traders because it represents a buildup of energy. As prices bounce between support and resistance, the market is gathering momentum for its next breakout—either upward in the case of a bullish breakout or downward in the case of a bearish breakout. The tight range during consolidation is particularly appealing for traders as it provides a clearer picture of where support and resistance lie, helping them plan precise entries and exits when the market finally makes its move.

The Importance of Consolidation

Consolidation phases are incredibly valuable for traders because they often serve as the foundation for some of the most recognizable and widely used patterns in technical analysis. Patterns like triangles, rectangles, and cup-and-handle formations typically emerge during periods of consolidation, giving traders a structured way to interpret the market's behavior. These patterns act as visual guides that help traders identify when the market is likely to break out of consolidation and in which direction it might move.

A narrowing price range can result in the formation of a triangle pattern, serving as a signal that a breakout is about to happen. Similarly, a rectangle pattern forms when price moves within a clearly defined horizontal range, providing an opportunity to catch the breakout once the price breaks through the upper or lower boundary of the rectangle.

One of the primary reasons to focus on consolidation is that the breakout following the consolidation is often strong and decisive. The consolidation phase allows the market to gather energy, resulting in a quick and powerful breakout that presents traders with high potential for rewards. The tight range of price movement also allows for setting smaller stop-losses, limiting risk exposure while maximizing the potential for profit.

What is Buildup in Pattern?

A buildup refers to a phase of tight consolidation within a larger consolidation pattern. Essentially, it is a period when the price fluctuates within a narrow range just before a breakout. This indicates that energy is being concentrated and a strong move is likely to follow once the consolidation phase ends. The tighter this range, the more explosive the eventual move tends to be. Think of a buildup as the market taking a deep breath before a significant price move. It is like the final tightening of tension before the price makes a powerful breakout from a technical pattern.

Buildups often occur right before the breakout of patterns such as Triangles, Rectangles, or Cup and Handle. What makes buildups particularly important is their ability to generate momentum-driven moves. Since the price range is so tight, traders can position themselves just before the breakout occurs, allowing them to take advantage of a strong and quick move. That is why experienced traders highly favor buildups within consolidation patterns when looking for powerful price action.

Personally, I prefer trading breakouts that come with a buildup because they tend to lead to momentum-based moves. A breakout from a buildup usually indicates that both buyers and sellers have reached an agreement, and once that narrow range is broken, the market tends to move swiftly in the breakout direction. As we delve into technical patterns like the Triangle, Rectangle, and Cup and Handle, I will provide examples of these patterns forming buildups. By identifying buildups within these formations, traders can anticipate strong moves and position themselves with minimal risk, making the buildup as a critical signal to watch for when preparing to enter a trade.

Triangle Pattern

A triangle is a continuation pattern that forms on a chart when the price of an asset moves within a converging range, creating a triangle-like shape. It represents a period of consolidation, after which the price is likely to continue moving in the direction of the prevailing trend. Traders look for these formations because they offer potential breakouts with strong momentum, especially when combined with buildup patterns.

Most times, triangles are continuation patterns, meaning that after the consolidation, the price will continue in the direction of the existing trend. For example, if the price is in an uptrend before the triangle forms, a breakout from the triangle will probably be bullish, continuing the upward movement. Conversely, in a downtrend, a breakout from a triangle often signals continuation of the downtrend.

Although triangles are primarily considered continuation patterns, they can sometimes act as reversal patterns, particularly if the triangle forms within a wedge pattern. For instance, in certain market conditions, a symmetrical triangle in a bullish trend can break downward, resulting in a bearish reversal. Traders need to be cautious of such scenarios, as these can lead to false breakouts, known as "traps," where the market briefly breaks out in one direction before sharply reversing.

There are three main types of triangle patterns in technical analysis:

1. **Ascending Triangle**

   The ascending triangle is generally seen as a bullish pattern. It forms when the price creates a series of higher lows while the resistance level remains constant. The repeated testing of resistance indicates growing bullish pressure, with buyers gradually pushing the price higher. The breakout from an ascending triangle usually results in an upward move, confirming the continuation of the uptrend. In a bearish market, this pattern can signal a potential reversal.

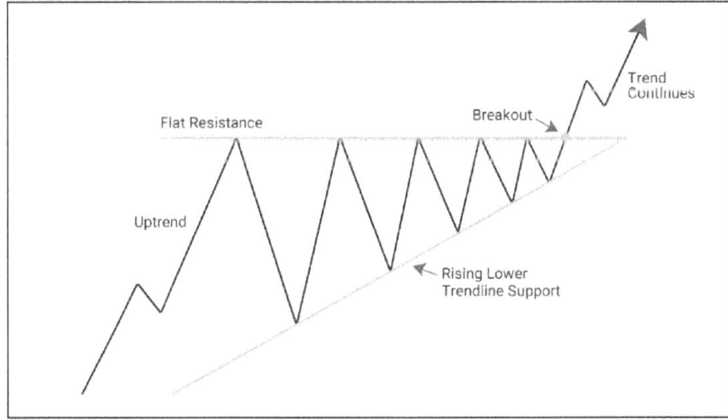

Figure 4.1: Image of Ascending Triangle

2. **Descending Triangle**

   The descending triangle is often a bearish pattern, formed when the price creates a series of lower highs while support remains constant. This suggests that sellers are gaining control, and a breakdown below the support level indicates a continuation of the downtrend. In a bullish market, the descending triangle can also act as a reversal pattern if a breakdown occurs.

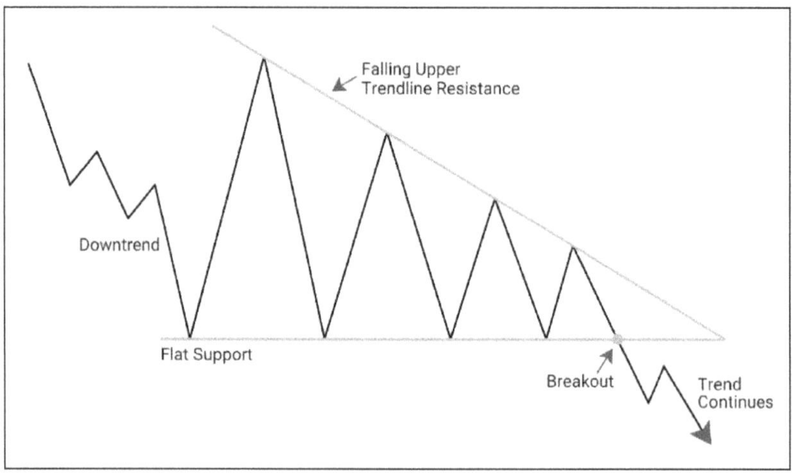

Figure 4.2: Image of Descending Triangle

3. **Symmetrical Triangle**

   The symmetrical triangle does not have a directional bias and is formed when the price converges between two trendlines, one sloping downward and the other sloping upward. This pattern reflects market indecision, where neither buyers nor sellers dominate. The breakout from a symmetrical triangle can go in either direction. In an uptrend, the breakout is more likely to be upward, while in a downtrend, the breakout is more likely to be downward.

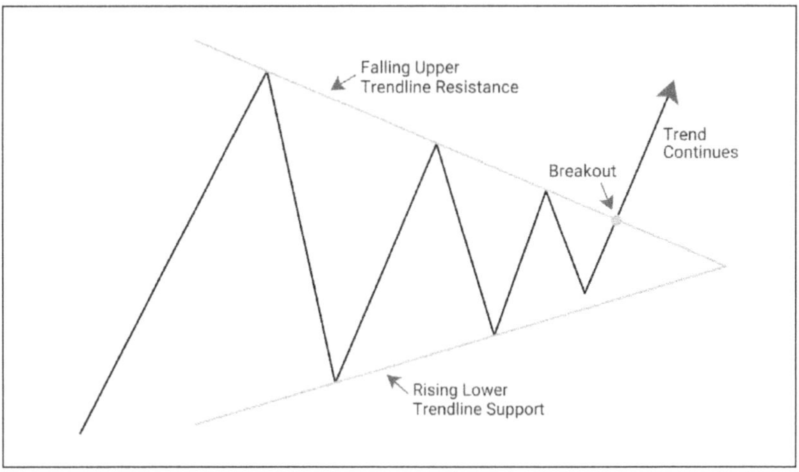

Figure 4.3: Image of Symmetrica Triangle

Participating in Triangle Patterns

Trading a triangle pattern is straightforward. When a candle breaks through the resistance level of a triangle, that candle becomes the breakout candle. Once the high of the breakout candle is breached, traders can confidently participate in the trade, expecting the price to follow through in the direction of the breakout.

- **Stop Loss:** Place the stop-loss below the low of the breakout candle to protect against false breakouts.
- **Target Calculation:** The target is determined by measuring the height of the triangle (the distance between the highest and lowest points of the triangle) and adding that to the high of the breakout candle. This projection helps set realistic profit targets based on the pattern's formation.

Case Study: 360 One Wam Ltd

In this case study, we observe the breakout of a triangle pattern on the chart of 360 ONE Ltd, which presented a promising trading opportunity. The triangle pattern, a classic continuation pattern in technical analysis, indicated a phase of consolidation or buildup where the stock price moved within converging trendlines, gradually forming lower highs and higher lows. This consolidation period reflects market indecision, where buyers and sellers were evenly matched. As the price tightened, it created the conditions for a breakout.

Figure 4.4: Formation of Ascending Triangle on daily timeframe Candlestick chart of 360ONE

On November 30, 2023, the stock price broke above the resistance level at 570, signaling the breakout from the triangle pattern. The breakout candle on that day reached a high of 580, marking an important reference point for the trade. On December 1, 2023, the breakout was confirmed as the price crossed the breakout candle's high, showing a continuation of the bullish trend.

To calculate the target for this trade, we use the height of the triangle pattern, which was 121.40 points. According to technical analysis principles, the target is calculated by adding the height of the triangle to the high of the breakout candle. In this case, the target is calculated as:

Target = High of Breakout Candle + Height of Triangle

Target = 580 + 121.40 = 701.40

The stock price continued to rise after the breakout, and the target of 701.40 was achieved on December 14, 2023, just 14 days after the breakout. During this period, the price followed a steady upward trend, offering traders a profitable opportunity.

Trade Summary Table:

Trade Detail	Value
Breakout Price	570
Breakout Candle High	580
Height of Triangle	121.40 points
Entry Price	580 (on breach of breakout candle high)
Target	701.4
Target Achieved Date	December 14, 2023
Total Trade Duration	14 days

Case Study: AIA Engineering Limited

AIA Engineering's recent price action provides a textbook example of the power of the Triangle Pattern with Buildup. The formation of the triangle pattern began on September 11, 2023, and continued through January 24, 2024. During this phase, the price oscillated within a tight range, marking clear levels of support and resistance as it converged towards the apex of the triangle. However, what makes this setup particularly noteworthy is the buildup phase that developed just before the breakout—a period of robust consolidation within the triangle.

This buildup phase is crucial in understanding the momentum potential of a breakout. In AIA Engineering's case, this period of buildup within the triangle acted as a "spring-loading" effect, concentrating market energy and setting the stage for an imminent and sharp price move. As the consolidation phase narrowed further within the larger triangle pattern, the price action indicated that a strong directional move was highly probable.

On January 24, 2024, the stock formed a breakout candle with a high of 3909, signalling the pattern's completion. The very next day, this breakout level was confirmed as the price breached the high of the breakout candle, giving traders a solid entry point aligned with the technical setup. With a triangle height of 476.85 points, the target was calculated by adding this height to the breakout level, establishing a price target that reflected the projected momentum generated by both the triangle and the buildup within it.

Figure 4.5: Formation of Ascending Triangle on daily timeframe Candlestick chart of AIAENG

What followed was a swift and rewarding movement. Within just five trading days, by February 1, 2024, the target was achieved. This rapid fulfillment of the target underscores the power of buildup within a triangle pattern. Unlike more traditional breakouts, the presence of a buildup can significantly enhance the likelihood of a swift move post-breakout, allowing traders to capture momentum-driven gains within a shorter time frame.

AIA Engineering's example highlights why patterns with buildup are so potent; the consolidation within the larger pattern acts as a pressure point, releasing energy in a burst once the breakout occurs. For traders, this means participating in trades where the risk is contained by the buildup and the reward is amplified by the swift momentum, all while maintaining clear and objective stop-loss and target levels.

Trade Summary Table:

Details	Description
Stock	AIA Engineering
Pattern	Triangle with Buildup
Triangle Formation Period	September 11, 2023 - January 24, 2024
Breakout Date	January 24, 2024
High of Breakout Candle	3909
Confirmation of Breakout	January 25, 2024
Triangle Height	476.85 points
Target Achieved Date	February 01, 2024
Days to Target	5 days
Trade Insight	Swiftly moving after a buildup, the breakout highlights strong potential for momentum.

Rectangle Pattern

The rectangle pattern is a commonly observed continuation pattern in technical analysis. It occurs when the price of an asset consolidates between two horizontal lines, which represent the levels of support and resistance. This consolidation creates a trading range, indicating a state of indecision or consolidation before a potential price breakout in line with the prevailing trend. The rectangle pattern is formed as the price oscillates within the defined support and resistance levels, forming a rectangular shape on the chart. This confinement suggests that the price is stuck within this range for a certain period. The duration of the consolidation is a crucial factor, as a longer consolidation period often leads to a more significant breakout. Traders typically watch for a breakout above the resistance level as a bullish signal, or a breakout below the support level as a bearish signal.

1. **Accumulation Phase**: During an uptrend, the rectangle may represent an accumulation phase, where market participants accumulate positions before the price breaks out to continue the uptrend.
2. **Distribution Phase**: In a downtrend, a rectangle pattern may represent a distribution phase, where sellers dominate, leading to a breakdown below the support level.

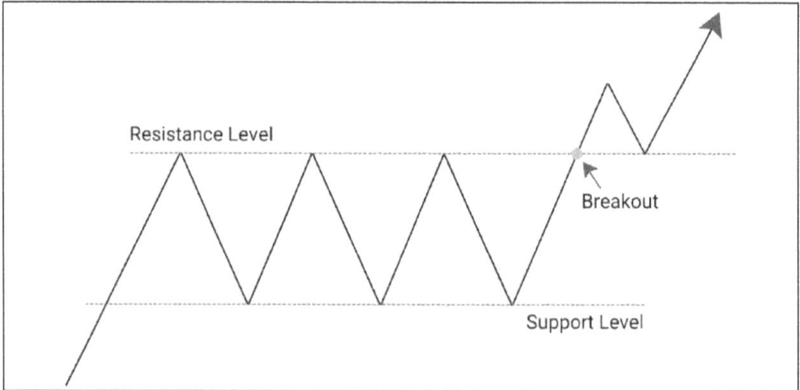

Figure 4.6: Image of Rectangle pattern

Participating in Rectangle Patterns

Trading a rectangle pattern is straightforward and similar to triangle patterns. When a candle breaks through the resistance of the rectangle, that candle becomes the breakout candle. Traders enter the trade once the high of this breakout candle is breached, indicating the beginning of a potential new trend.

- **Stop Loss**: Place the stop-loss below the low of the breakout candle.
- **Target Calculation**: The target is calculated by measuring the height of the rectangle pattern (the distance between support and resistance) and adding this height to the high of the breakout candle.

Case Study: TVS Motors Limited

Figure 4.7: Formation of rectangle pattern on daily timeframe Candlestick chart of TVSMOTOR

In this case study, we explore the rectangle pattern that formed on the chart of TVS Motor Company Ltd, where the stock price consolidated in a well-defined range before eventually breaking out.

The rectangle pattern emerged as the price moved between two horizontal lines: the support at the lower boundary and the resistance at the upper boundary. The price remained within this range for a considerable period, forming the rectangle. The breakout of the rectangle pattern initially occurred on July 23, 2023, but the breakout failed to gain momentum, and the price fell back into the consolidation range, invalidating the breakout.

Finally, on August 30, 2023, a strong breakout candle formed, which decisively broke through the upper resistance of the rectangle. The high of the breakout candle on August 30 was 1421. Following the established rules for participating in the breakout of a rectangle pattern, the trade entry was triggered when the high of the breakout candle was breached on August 31, 2023.

The height of the rectangle, measuring 99.70 points, was added to the high of the breakout candle (1421) to calculate the target. This gives a target of 1421 + 99.70 = 1520.70. The target was achieved on September 18, 2023, marking the end of the trade.

The total number of days in the trade was 18 days from the breakout confirmation on August 31 to the target achievement on September 18. This case study illustrates how the rectangle pattern can provide a clear and actionable trade setup, with the breakout and target calculation based on the measured move principle.

Trade Summary Table:

Trade Detail	Value
Breakout Date	August 30, 2023
Breakout Candle High	1421
Breakout Confirmation Date	August 31, 2023
Rectangle Height	99.70 points
Target Price	1520.7
Target Achievement Date	September 18, 2023
Number of Days in Trade	18 days

Case Study: Cholamandalam Investment and Finance Company Limited

The case of Cholamandalam Investment and Finance Company Limited (CHOLAFIN) illustrates the combined power of the Rectangle Pattern with Buildup in generating strong post-breakout moves. This setup unfolded over an extended period, with CHOLAFIN forming a clear rectangle pattern from August 23, 2022, to April 6, 2023. During this period, the stock oscillated within a horizontal range, establishing defined levels of support and resistance, signaling a period of consolidation.

The rectangle pattern, with a height of 133 points, represented a balanced struggle between buyers and sellers. The breakout finally occurred on April 6, 2023, when the stock surged above the resistance level, forming a breakout candle with a high of 847. This candle marked the end of the rectangle pattern, signaling that the stock was primed for a directional move. However, the presence of a subsequent buildup phase added a unique strength to this setup, enhancing the likelihood of a successful breakout continuation.

Figure 4.8: Formation of rectangle pattern on daily timeframe Candlestick chart of CHOLAFIN

After the breakout on April 6, the stock entered a tight consolidation, or "buildup" phase, from April 6 to April 27, 2023. This buildup phase within the broader rectangle breakout served as an additional confirmation of buyer commitment, where the price held steadily near the breakout level without falling back into the previous range. This consolidation provided traders with a lower-risk entry, confirming that the breakout was not a false move, but rather a precursor to a sustained uptrend.

The breakout became actionable on April 10, 2023, when the price breached the high of the breakout candle. By setting a target based on the height of the rectangle pattern, traders anticipated a move of 133 points above the breakout level, translating to a target price of 980. The buildup's presence signaled the accumulation of buying interest at higher levels, creating a foundation for a stronger, quicker move towards the target.

True to the pattern's strength, the target was achieved on May 5, 2023, just under a month after the initial breakout confirmation. The combination of the rectangle breakout and subsequent buildup led to a steady, momentum-driven move, offering traders a solid opportunity to capture gains with a clearly defined risk level. This case underscores the power of buildups following breakouts, especially in rectangle patterns where the buildup confirms and accelerates the anticipated move.

Trade Summary Table:

Details	Description
Stock	CHOLAFIN
Pattern	Rectangle with Buildup
Rectangle Formation Period	August 23, 2022 - April 6, 2023
Breakout Date	April 6, 2023
High of Breakout Candle	847
Confirmation of Breakout	April 10, 2023
Rectangle Height	133 points
Target Price	980
Target Achieved Date	May 5, 2023
Days to Target	25 days
Trade Insight	Rectangle breakout followed by a buildup, allowing for a strong, sustained move with controlled risk

Cup and Handle Pattern

The cup and handle pattern is a bullish continuation pattern that indicates a possible continuation of an uptrend following a consolidation phase. This pattern forms when the price undergoes a significant, rounded consolidation (the cup), followed by a smaller retracement (the handle), before finally breaking out. The cup and handle pattern is named as such because it resembles the shape of a tea cup, with the cup representing a rounded bottom and the handle symbolizing a brief consolidation before a breakout.

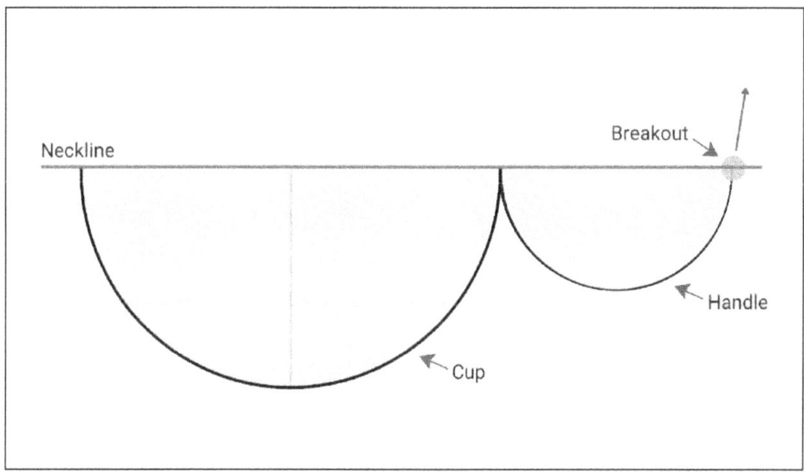

Figure 4.9: Image of Cup & Handle Pattern

The Cup and the Handle

1. **The Cup:** The cup represents a rounding bottom, often following a downtrend or a consolidation phase. This is the period where the asset consolidates after a prolonged move, forming a "U" shape. A deep, well-rounded cup is generally seen as more bullish, as it indicates a long period of accumulation.

2. **The Handle:** After the cup is formed, the handle appears as a small consolidation or pullback before the breakout. The handle typically slopes downwards, representing a brief period of profit-taking or uncertainty before buyers push the price

higher. The breakout from the handle signals the continuation of the bullish trend.

Key Points to Remember

- **Length**: The longer and more "U"-shaped the cup, the stronger the signal. Shallow or "V"-shaped cups are considered weaker.
- **Depth**: The depth of the handle should be relatively shallow compared to the depth of the cup. Ideally, the handle should form in the upper half of the cup.
- **Volume**: During the formation of the cup, volume tends to decrease. As the price moves higher, back to test previous highs, the volume should increase, confirming the strength of the pattern.

Participating in Cup and Handle Patterns

Trading the cup and handle pattern is straightforward. Once the price breaks above the resistance level of the handle, the candle that breaks this level becomes the breakout candle. Traders enter the trade when the high of this breakout candle is breached, signaling the continuation of the uptrend.

- **Stop Loss**: Place the stop-loss below the low of the handle, as this is the final consolidation phase before the breakout.
- **Target Calculation**: The target is calculated by measuring the height of the cup (the distance from the low of the cup to the resistance) and adding this height to the breakout point above the handle.

Case Study: J. B. Chemicals & Pharmaceuticals Limited

In the case of J.B. Chemicals & Pharmaceuticals Limited (JBCHEPHARM), a classic cup and handle pattern formed between October and December 2023, signaling a potential continuation of the prevailing uptrend. The cup component of the pattern developed as the stock's price first experienced a rounded decline, reaching its lowest point in early November 2023. Following this low, the price gradually recovered, completing the "cup" by mid-December. The pattern's handle formed soon after, as the price entered a brief period of consolidation, allowing the stock to gather momentum for the next move.

Figure 4.10: Formation of Cup & Handle pattern on daily timeframe Candlestick chart of JBCHEPHARM

The breakout from this cup and handle pattern occurred on December 22, 2023, when the price broke above the resistance level with a breakout candle, reaching a high of 1631. As per our strategy, the breakout was confirmed on December 26, 2023, when the price surpassed the high of the breakout candle, signaling a strong upward movement and a confirmation of the breakout.

The height of the cup was measured at 285.85 points, which is the difference between the cup's lowest point and the resistance level. To calculate the target, this height was added to the high of the breakout candle (1631), resulting in a target price of 1916.85.

The stock reached the calculated target of 1916.85 on February 7, 2024, confirming the validity of the cup and handle pattern. This trade took a total of 47 days from the breakout confirmation to the target achievement, and it provided traders with a well-structured, low-risk opportunity to capitalize on the upward momentum.

Trade Summary Table:

Trade Detail	Values
Breakout Date	December 22, 2023
Breakout Candle High	1631
Breakout Confirmation Date	December 26, 2023
Cup Height	285.85
Target	1916.85
Target Achievement Date	February 7, 2024
Number of Days in Trade	47 Days

Science of Trailing Stop-loss

There are several effective ways to trail stop-losses in technical analysis, each offering a balance between capturing profits and protecting capital. Trailing stop-loss methods allow traders to follow the trend while having a predefined exit point as the trade progresses. Let's break down three widely used methods for trailing stop-loss: Using Moving Average, SuperTrend, and the 3 Candlestick Exit.

Using Moving Average

Once a trade is entered, and the price starts moving in the desired direction, one of the most reliable ways to manage the position is by using a moving average as a trailing stop. Specifically, Exponential Moving Averages (EMA), like the 9 EMA or 21 EMA, are often employed for this purpose. The basic idea is to allow the trade to continue as long as the price stays above the moving average in a long trade or below the moving average in a short trade.

However, relying solely on an EMA can sometimes cause premature exits due to minor pullbacks, leading to fake outs. To avoid this, the **2-Candlestick Rule** is implemented as a safeguard. Here is how it works:

- The first candle must close below the EMA (in a long trade).
- The exit is triggered only if the next candle closes below the close of the first candle.

This provides a buffer, ensuring that traders do not exit too early due to small price fluctuations. The 9 EMA is typically used for shorter holding periods, allowing for quicker exits. However, if a trader wants to hold the position for a longer time, the 21 EMA can be used. The choice of EMA largely depends on the trader's style and the market's volatility. This method allows for a systematic and objective exit strategy. Traders can set up scanners that flag stocks when the price closes below the EMA, providing an efficient way to monitor trades across multiple stocks.

Figure 4.11: Daily timeframe Candlestick chart of CHOLAFIN along with 9-period EMA

In this example of Cholamandalam Investment and Finance Company (CHOLAFIN), a rectangle pattern breakout provided an initial target of 982. Instead of exiting at the fixed target, we decided to employ the 9 EMA trailing stop-loss method to capture potentially larger gains. This approach allowed us to maximize the trade's profitability by riding the ongoing trend rather than taking profits at the predefined target.

After the breakout on April 6, CHOLAFIN continued its upward trend, remaining consistently above the 9 EMA. This moving average served as a dynamic support level, guiding us in the trend and allowing us to stay in the position as long as the price closed above it. Following the 9 EMA trailing stop-loss rule, we held the position until a clear signal to exit was triggered.

The exit occurred when two consecutive candles closed below the 9 EMA, signaling that the trend might be weakening. This trailing stop-loss approach allowed us to exit at 1090, significantly above the initial target of 982. By following the 9 EMA, we captured a gain of 238 points instead of the originally anticipated 130 points—an additional profit of 108 points, demonstrating how trailing stops can help traders ride strong trends to maximize returns.

The chart clearly shows how the 9 EMA trailed along the trend, providing a flexible yet disciplined exit strategy. The result was a substantial profit, showcasing the benefits of a trailing stop-loss approach in strong trending stocks.

Using SuperTrend

The SuperTrend indicator is another powerful tool for trailing stop-losses. It adjusts according to price movements and volatility, allowing for dynamic stop placement. When market volatility is high, the SuperTrend stop-loss will widen, giving the trade more room to breathe. Conversely, in low-volatility conditions, it tightens the stop-loss, protecting against adverse moves.

SuperTrend works by calculating a stop-loss based on the asset's volatility, ensuring that the stop adjusts based on the current market environment. Traders often use SuperTrend when they want a trailing stop that moves in tandem with market conditions, offering flexibility while still protecting profits. The adaptability of the SuperTrend indicator makes it particularly useful in trending markets, where prices are subject to swings in volatility.

This indicator, much like the Moving Average, can be used alongside other technical tools to ensure traders are not exiting prematurely.

In this example, we revisit our case study of TVS Motors, where a rectangle pattern breakout was initially used to set a fixed target. However, instead of taking profits at the calculated target based on the height of the rectangle, we could have used a trailing stop loss (TSL) with the SuperTrend indicator to stay in the trade longer and capture additional gains as the stock continued to rally.

Upon the rectangle pattern breakout, we entered the trade on the breach of the breakout candle high. As the price moved in our favor, we set the SuperTrend indicator as our trailing stop-loss guide. This allowed us to ride the uptrend without manually adjusting the stop with every price fluctuation. The SuperTrend indicator adjusted itself according to the stock's volatility, staying further from the price when volatility was high and closer during quieter market phases.

Instead of exiting at the initial target, the SuperTrend kept us in the trade for an extended period, capturing approximately 47% in gains. The SuperTrend finally flipped to a bearish signal, indicating an exit point, which locked in significant profits. This approach allowed us to capitalize on the extended rally rather than exiting prematurely at a fixed target, demonstrating the potential of trailing stops to maximize gains.

Figure 4.12: Daily timeframe Candlestick chart of TVSMOTOR along with SuperTrend

By employing a trailing stop loss with the SuperTrend, we could stay in the trade for a much longer period, taking advantage of the prolonged uptrend. This method provided a structured and automated way to protect gains and minimize downside risk, especially useful in trending markets like we saw with TVS Motors.

However, it is important to recognize that trailing stop-losses may not always lead to exits at higher prices compared to a fixed target. There will be instances where the trailing stop-loss triggers an exit below the fixed target, or when the stock briefly touches the target before reversing and hitting the trailing stop. In such cases, it is natural to feel a bit of regret for not locking in profits at the initial target.

This approach, while highly effective in capturing extended trends, is not infallible and will not always yield higher profits. Markets can be unpredictable, and there will be times when trailing stop-losses work against us by exiting too early during brief pullbacks. Despite this, I personally favor the trailing stop-loss method, as it provides the opportunity to capture an ongoing trend to its fullest extent. The potential to ride a strong trend outweighs the occasional missed profit, making it a valuable approach for those looking to stay in trades longer and maximize gains from persistent trends.

Using 3 Candlestick Exit

The 3 Candlestick Exit strategy is a simple yet highly effective method for trailing stop-losses. It is especially useful in markets where there are frequent breakouts followed by sharp reversals, as it keeps the stop-loss tight, allowing traders to lock in profits before the market turns against them.

Here is how it works:

- In a long trade, the stop-loss is placed at the lowest low of the last three candles.
- In a short trade, the stop-loss is set at the highest high of the last three candles.

As each new candle forms, the stop-loss is adjusted, following the price movement. This ensures that the stop-loss moves closer to the current price during strong trends, allowing the trade to capture more profits. However, as soon as the market starts consolidating or reversing, the position is closed, locking in the gains made during the trend.

Figure 4.13: Daily timeframe Candlestick chart of JBCHEPHARM

This method offers the advantage of tracking price action very closely, which means traders are less likely to give up significant profits due to market reversals. The 3 Candlestick Exit works exceptionally well in volatile markets, where prices often experience quick reversals after breakout moves.

In this example, we used AIA Engineering (AIAENG) to demonstrate the effectiveness of the 3 Candle Rule as a trailing stop-loss method. Initially, we set a fixed target based on the pattern breakout, which was achieved. However, we continued to follow the trend using the 3 Candle Rule to capture additional gains beyond the fixed target.

The 3 Candle Rule works by setting the stop-loss at the lowest point of the last three candles. If this level is breached, we immediately exit the trade. This allows us to retain a significant portion of the gains without risking a full retracement.

Using a trailing stop-loss has its strengths. It allows traders to stay in the trade as long as the momentum is favorable, while also providing an exit point if the trend starts to reverse. The 3 Candle Rule is especially effective in markets with sharp moves and quick reversals. It helps traders lock in profits without waiting for a potentially delayed signal.

Although it may not guarantee the highest possible exit, the 3 Candle Rule strikes a balance between capturing gains and managing risk, as shown in this AIA Engineering trade.

In conclusion, using trailing stop-loss techniques is essential for managing trades effectively and protecting profits. Whether you prefer a smooth approach like the Moving Average, a dynamic one like the SuperTrend, or a price-action-based method like the 3 Candlestick Exit, these strategies offer a structured way to trail your stop and exit trades at optimal points.

Conclusion

In this chapter, we have explored consolidation, buildups, and trailing stop-loss techniques—the key components that empower traders to effectively manage risk and maximize returns. Understanding these concepts goes beyond simple price movements; they represent the underlying psychology of the market, a battle between buyers and sellers where patience and timing are crucial.

Consolidation patterns like triangles, rectangles, and the cup and handle provide powerful setups for traders looking to capitalize on breakout opportunities. Each pattern offers its own set of rules and characteristics, but the principle remains the same—recognizing a period of indecision in the market and positioning yourself to capture the next significant move.

However, as we have seen, it is not just about identifying the patterns—it is about managing the trade through proper position sizing and smart exit strategies. This is where trailing stop-loss techniques, such as the

9 EMA rule, the dynamic SuperTrend, or the precise 3-Candlestick Exit, come into play. They allow you to secure profits while reducing the emotional strain of trading, keeping your strategy consistent and objective.

Ultimately, the goal is to protect your capital while allowing your winners to run, and these techniques provide the necessary structure to achieve just that. By applying these tools in conjunction with the chart patterns discussed, you can create a robust and adaptable trading plan—one that not only helps you identify potential entry points but also safeguards your hard-earned profits.

As I have demonstrated with case studies and practical examples, these concepts are not theoretical—they can be implemented in real-world scenarios to enhance your trading performance. Whether it is the breakout of a triangle, rectangle, or a cup and handle, these patterns and trailing methods give you an edge in the market, allowing you to participate in significant moves while minimizing risk.

In the next chapters, we will continue to build on these technical principles, delving deeper into more advanced trading techniques. But for now, mastering consolidation and buildups, combined with intelligent trailing stop management, gives you the foundation needed for long-term success in the markets.

TRADE USING DARVAS BOX THEORY

• •

When I first entered the realm of technical analysis, the Darvas Box theory made a significant impact on me and it was one of the earliest theories I learnt about. Nicolas Darvas, the man behind this strategy, is a figure who continues to inspire traders around the world, including myself. What stands out about Darvas is not just his method, but the incredible determination and resourcefulness he demonstrated in an era when trading was far from easy.

Imagine trading in the 1950s—a time when the technology we take for granted today did not exist. There were no sophisticated software programs to track 52-week highs, calculate ATRs, or manage a portfolio's technical data. Darvas, however, managed to do all of this manually. He meticulously tracked stock prices, calculated highs and lows, and maintained records with incredible precision. This, in itself, is a powerful lesson in dedication and discipline. If we truly want to succeed in trading and investing, we must be prepared to put in the effort that success demands, just as Darvas did.

What fascinated me most about Darvas was his pioneering approach to system trading. He might have been the first trader I read about who emphasized on the importance of having a clear, rule-based trading system. The Darvas Box strategy is a testament to this approach, with well-defined entry, exit, and stop-loss conditions. Darvas consistently emphasized the necessity of following a system in his book. He believed, and rightly so, that systematic trading is what enables consistent success in the stock markets.

As we delve into the Darvas Box strategy in this chapter, keep in mind the lessons that Darvas taught us—not just about the mechanics of trading, but about the mindset and dedication required to be a successful trader. His story is not just about a method; it is about the unwavering commitment to discipline and systematic trading that led to his remarkable success.

The Origin of Darvas Box Theory

Born in 1920 in Hungary, the turbulence in Europe shaped Nicolas Darvas's early life, as it was on the brink of World War II. Although he studied economics at the University of Budapest, Darvas's true passion was dance. As the war escalated, he fled his homeland, eventually making his way to the United States in the 1940s. He and his half-sister Julia became a dance duo called "Darvas and Julia." They wowed audiences around the world with their elegant and athletic performances. His globe-trotting lifestyle heavily influenced his unique approach, far from the financial hubs of the world.

Despite his success in dance, Darvas developed a growing interest in the stock market. His first foray into investing came in 1952, when he purchased shares in a Canadian company on a whim, with no concrete strategy. This initial experiment resulted in a modest profit, fueling a curiosity that rapidly became an obsession. Unlike numerous investors of his time, Darvas did not involve himself in the daily grind of Wall Street. Since he lived a nomadic lifestyle, he could only rely on weekly issues of Barron's for stock information. By distancing himself from the market's constant noise, he could concentrate on long-term trends, which formed the basis of his trading philosophy.

As Darvas continued to tour and perform, he used the limited data available to him—mainly stock prices and volume—to study market movements from afar. This specific point of view inspired him to create what would eventually become the Darvas Box Theory. Darvas differentiated his method from other technical analysis approaches by prioritizing broader trends over daily market fluctuations, which typically emphasizes real-time data.

By the late 1950s, Darvas had refined his method, blending technical analysis with a psychological understanding of market behavior. He knew that market movements were not solely based on economic fundamentals, but also on how investors felt and acted. Drawing from his experience as a stage performer, Darvas understood the importance of timing and how trends in the markets and popular culture can influence things.

Darvas achieved his biggest trading success from 1957 to 1959, turning $10,000 into more than $2 million. His success did not go unnoticed. In 1959, *Time* magazine, one of the most influential publications of that era, featured Darvas in an article that highlighted not only his achievements but also the booming stock market of the time, which had surged over 50% in the previous two years as measured by the S&P 500.

This recognition catapulted Darvas and his theory into the spotlight, and his book *"How I Made $2,000,000 in the Stock Market"* became a bestseller. The book gives readers a look into the mind of a dancer-turned-investor who successfully outsmarted the market using discipline, observation, and a unique approach to stock trading.

Darvas's Principles for Identifying Stocks

Nicolas Darvas had his own set of principles for choosing stocks, along with the technical rules of the Darvas Box Theory. By rooting these principles in both fundamental analysis and market psychology, Nicolas Darvas could identify stocks with the highest potential for success. Here are the guiding principles Darvas used:

1. **Focus on Companies with Promising Growth and Earnings Prospects**

   Darvas prioritized buying companies whose growth and earnings prospects appeared very promising. In his opinion, a stock's sustained upward movement relied on strong fundamentals. Companies that had solid earnings growth, innovative products, and a strong market position generally experienced stock price growth over time.

2. **Align with the Overall Market Trend**

   Before entering a trade, Darvas would assess the broader market trend to ensure that stocks were in an uptrend. He understood that even the strongest stocks could encounter difficulties in a declining market, so he emphasized the importance of aligning with the market's overall momentum. This approach helped him avoid potential losses in bearish environments.

3. **Select Stocks from Strong Industries or Groups**

   Darvas understood the importance of industry strength in stock selection. He looked for stocks from strong industries or groups, as these sectors were more likely to outperform in market uptrends. Darvas increased his chances of finding successful trades by focusing on leaders in top sectors.

4. **Ensure Price Breakout with High Volume**

   Darvas's strategy involved using above-average trading volume to confirm a price breakout. The surge in volume suggests high market interest and raises the chances of a continued upward trend following the breakout. Darvas was hesitant to enter a trade without this confirmation.

Darvas used these principles to find stocks that had high potential for gains and low risk from market volatility. These guidelines and the technical aspects of the Darvas Box Theory formed the foundation of Darvas' trading strategy.

Understanding the Darvas Box

The Darvas Box visually represents price movements and is a tool that helps traders identify potential breakout and breakdown points in the market. Darvas believes that stocks typically trade within a specific range, referred to as a "box," before undergoing a significant move either upwards or downwards. Below are the key components and steps involved in applying the Darvas Box Theory:

Box Formation

Darvas identified stocks trading within a narrow price range, forming a "box" on the price chart. Drawing horizontal lines at the upper and lower boundaries of the recent trading range delineates this box. These boundaries represent the resistance and support levels. Below are the detailed steps to plot a Darvas Box:

- **Stock Crossing 52-Week High**

  Darvas favored participating in a stock when it crossed its 52-week high, indicating strong positive sentiment. However, to refine this rule, instead of looking at the 52-week high, we consider the stock's 250-day high. This modification aligns with the estimated number of trading days in a year, enabling a more accurate and timely analysis. Therefore, the first rule is that a stock must break its last 250-day high to be considered for the Darvas Box. This breakout signals that the stock has positive momentum and market sentiment.

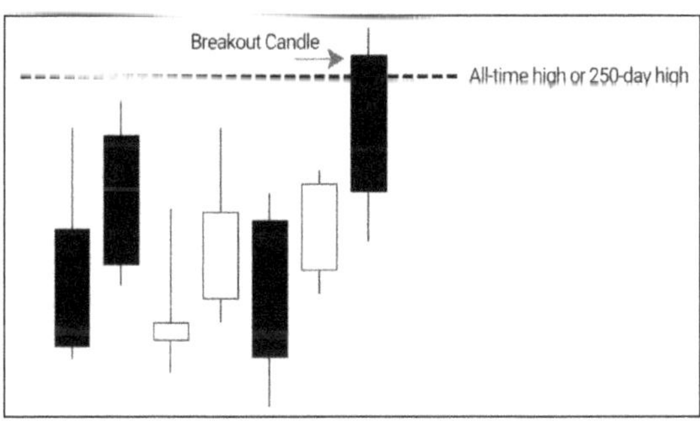

Figure 5.1: Image of Breakout Candle

- **Marking the Box**

  Once a stock breaks its 250-day high, the next step is to identify the "ceiling" and "floor" of the Darvas Box.

  - **Ceiling Formation**

    To determine the ceiling, identify the candle that breaks the 250-day high. This breakout candle must maintain its high for the next three trading days, meaning that during these three days, the price should trade below the breakout candle's high. This ensures that the breakout is genuine and not a short-lived spike. It's important to note that the price may continue to rise after the breakout without retracing right away. However, the key is that the breakout candle's high remains unchallenged for three consecutive days. When this condition is met, we mark the high of this breakout candle as the ceiling.

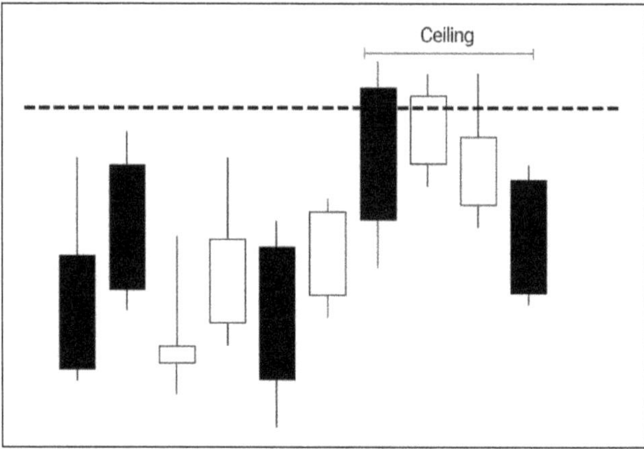

Figure 5.2: Image of Ceiling Formation

  - **Floor Formation**

    After establishing the ceiling, the next step is to identify the floor. The floor is marked by finding a candle whose low remains protected for the next three trading days, meaning that the price does not fall below this low during this period. Once the price trades above this low for three consecutive days, the low of this candle is marked as the floor.

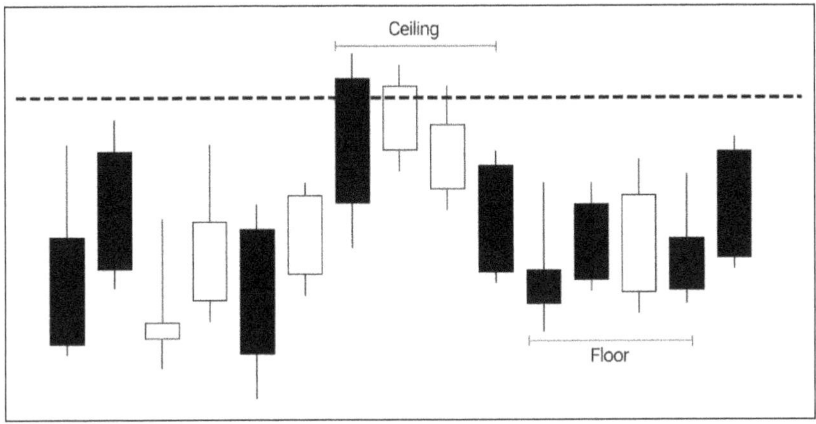

Figure 5.3: Image of Floor Formation

- ○ **Completing the Darvas Box**
  With the ceiling and floor identified, draw horizontal lines from the high of the ceiling and the low of the floor to form the Darvas Box. This box visually represents the price range within which the stock is trading, setting the stage for potential breakout or breakdown points.

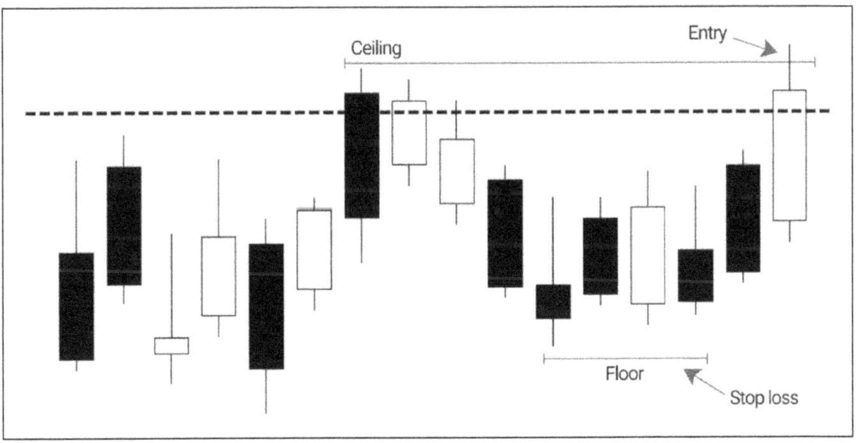

Figure 5.4: Image of Box Formation

Just in case, if the existing ceiling is breached before forming a floor, new ceiling will be marked. Similarly, if the existing floor is breached before giving the breakout from the box, the new floor is marked. The process of updating the ceilings and floors continues until the price gives a breakout from the box.

Volume Confirmation

Volume plays a crucial role in confirming the validity of a breakout or breakdown from the box. According to Darvas, a significant move should have increased trading volume, whether it is above or below the boundaries. This volume surge serves as confirmation of the move's strength, indicating that the price action is supported by widespread market participation.

Buy Signal

When the price breaks above the top of the box and the trading volume is higher than average, Darvas sees it as a signal to buy. Darvas would initiate a buy position capitalizing on the upward momentum. The logic here is that a breakout from the box suggests a new upward trend, offering a profitable entry point for the trader.

Sell Signal

When the stock price falls below the lower boundary of the box, particularly if this breakdown is accompanied by increased volume, it triggers a sell signal. This movement suggests a potential reversal or breakdown, prompting Darvas to sell his position. Exiting the trade at this point helps avoid larger losses that could result from a sustained downward trend.

Stop-Loss Placement

To manage risk, Darvas employed a strict stop-loss strategy. He would place a stop-loss order just below the lower boundary of the box. If the stock price fell back into the box, this would indicate a potential false breakout. In such a scenario, Darvas would exit the trade to limit losses, adhering to the principle of preserving capital.

Trailing the Box

Darvas often identified himself as a "pilot trader," a label he used to depict his prudent, yet calculated, approach to acquiring market positions. After receiving a buy signal from a box breakout, Darvas would initiate a position. As the stock continued to form new boxes, he would trail his stop-loss to the floor of each newly established Darvas Box. Simultaneously, he would add fresh quantities to his position with each new breakout, cleverly pyramiding his investment.

Considerations and Risks

While the Darvas Box method has gained popularity and proven successful for some traders, it is important to recognize that no trading strategy is foolproof. The effectiveness of the Darvas Box can vary depending on market conditions, and, like any trading strategy, it comes with inherent risks.

You should use the Darvas Box as part of a comprehensive trading plan, integrating other technical and fundamental analysis to enhance your chances of success. Moreover, risk management techniques such as strict adherence to stop-losses and position sizing are crucial components of using this method effectively.

This approach offered two key advantages:

1. **Pyramiding on Strength**: By adding to his position as the trade moved in his favor, Darvas capitalized on the stock's growing strength. Each new box formation and breakout signaled increasing momentum, allowing him to build a larger position in a winning trade.
2. **Minimized Risk**: If the trade failed, the stop-loss set at the floor of the most recent Darvas Box limited potential losses.

This strategy protected his trading capital, ensuring that any setbacks did not significantly impact his overall portfolio.

This method allowed Darvas to maximize gains while carefully managing risk, reinforcing the disciplined approach that was central to his trading philosophy.

Summarizing Rules for Creating Stock Universe

Principle	Description	Objective Criteria
Growth and Earnings Prospects	Darvas prioritized companies with strong growth and earnings potential, knowing that solid fundamentals are key for sustaining price growth.	Select companies whose Profit After Tax (PAT) has improved over the last two financial years.
Overall Market Trend	Aligning with the overall market trend is crucial. Darvas recognized that even fundamentally strong stocks could struggle in a bearish environment. Ensuring that the broader market is in an uptrend increases the odds of success.	Ensure the stock's price is trading above the 200-period EMA on Daily charts, indicating alignment with the market uptrend.
Industry or Group Strength	Darvas believed in the strength of leading industries. Stocks within strong sectors outperform, especially during market uptrends.	Evaluate the Relative Strength (RS) of the stock versus the Nifty 50 index to confirm it belongs to a leading industry.

| Price Breakout with Volume | For a breakout to be meaningful, it must be supported by strong trading volume. Darvas used volume as a key confirmation of market interest, which helps to validate the breakout and reduce the risk of a false signal. | Plot the volume data with the 50-period EMA. The breakout volume should be above this average line, confirming the strength of the movement. |

Summarizing Rules for Marking Darvas Box

Rule	Description
Marking the Box: Ceiling	Identify the candle that breaks the 250-day high. If the high remains intact for the next 3 trading days (price trades below this high), mark it as the ceiling.
Marking the Box: Floor	Identify a candle that ensures the low remains protected for the next 3 trading days (where the price does not fall below this low). Mark this low as the floor.
Stop-Loss Placement	Place the initial stop-loss just below the floor of the Darvas Box to limit potential losses if the price falls back into the box.
Trailing Stop-Loss	As new boxes form and the price rises, trail the stop-loss to the floor of the most recent Darvas Box to lock in profits while allowing the trade to continue upward.
Enter a Trade	Buy the stock when its price breaks above the Darvas Box ceiling with high trading volume, indicating a new upward trend.
Exit a Trade	If the price falls below the Darvas Box floor with increased volume, consider exiting as it could indicate a potential reversal or trend failure.

Case Study: Blue Dart Express Ltd

In this case study, we will delve into the effective application of the Darvas Box Theory to Blue Dart Express Ltd. (BLUEDART). We will look at how the trade started with a 250-day breakout, study each Darvas Box that followed, and then summarize how the trade performed.

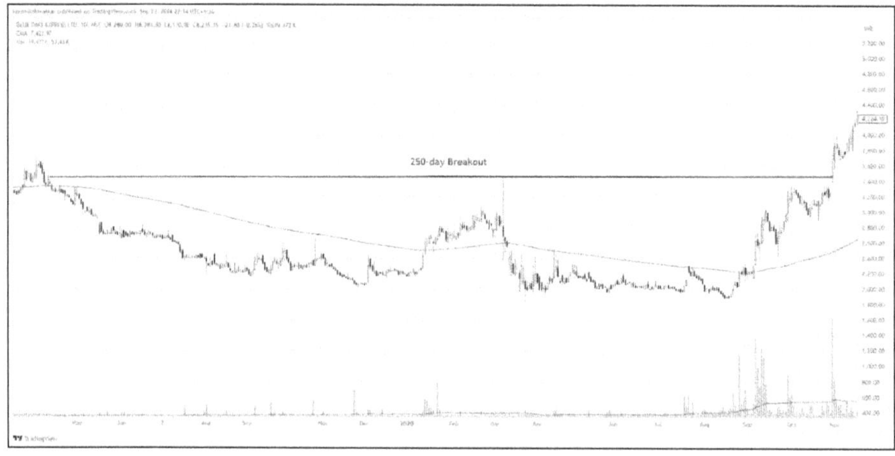

Figure 5.5: Marking of 250-day breakout on daily timeframe Candlestick chart of BLUEDART

On November 12, 2020, the journey started with a notable 250-day breakout at a price of 3465. This breakout marked a pivotal moment, signaling the start of a potential uptrend as the stock moved above a long-standing resistance level. The breakout was accompanied by higher-than-average volume, confirming the strength of this move and signaling a clear entry point according to the Darvas Box Theory.

Following the initial breakout, the stock started creating a sequence of Darvas Boxes, each marked by a resistance level (Ceiling) and a support level (Floor). The first Darvas Box saw a Ceiling forming at 3994 on November 03, 2020, and a Floor established at 3680 on November 05, 2020.

Figure 5.6: Marking of Darvas Box on daily timeframe candlestick chart of
BLUEDART

The breakout above the Ceiling occurred on November 12, 2020, just nine days after the Ceiling was formed, with strong volume confirming the bullish trend and continuation of the uptrend.

As the stock continued its upward trajectory, the second Darvas Box formed with a Ceiling at 4299.80 on November 17, 2020, and a Floor at 3709 on December 22, 2020. The stock remained in a consolidation phase for 36 days before breaking out of the Ceiling on January 22, 2021. This breakout was also supported by strong volume, further solidifying the stock's ongoing strength and the validity of the Darvas Box strategy.

A Ceiling at 4170 characterized the third Darvas Box on January 25, 2021, and a Floor at 3820 on February 01, 2021. This time, the stock broke out of the Ceiling on February 09, 2021, just nine days after forming the Ceiling. The quick breakout once again indicated strong bullish momentum, and the volume remained supportive of the price action.

With a Ceiling at 4949 on February 17, 2021, and a Floor set at 4501 on February 23, 2021, the fourth Darvas Box showed interesting movement. The stock broke out of this Ceiling on March 08, 2021, 19 days after the Ceiling was formed. The breakout continued with strong volume, confirming the uptrend.

The Ceiling of the fifth Darvas Box was set at 5845 on March 31, 2021, and the Floor was established at 4952 on April 26, 2021. This time, the stock took 49 days to break out above the Ceiling, finally doing so on May 19, 2021. The breakout from the fifth box took more time than usual, but the uptrend continued with significant volume, affirming the strength of the bullish move.

In the sixth Darvas Box, a Ceiling was formed at 6177.50 on May 27, 2021, and a Floor at 5306.50 on August 11, 2021. The stock stayed within this range for a considerable period, finally breaking out above the Ceiling on September 03, 2021, after 100 days. Despite the long consolidation, the breakout was solid, supported by strong volume, suggesting that the stock had gathered sufficient strength to continue its upward move.

Finally, the seventh Darvas Box formed with a Ceiling at 6544 on September 09, 2021, and a Floor at 6176 on September 21, 2021. Just nine days after establishing the Ceiling, the stock broke out above it on September 30, 2021. However, this would be the final breakout before the stock lost momentum.

When the price fell below the Floor of the seventh Darvas Box at 6176 on October 21, 2021, it triggered the exit point for this trade. The total trade duration was 343 days, from the initial entry on November 12, 2020, to the exit on October 21, 2021. During this period, the trade captured a significant move from 3465 to 6176, resulting in a gain of 2711 points. In percentage terms, the total gain from this trade was approximately 78.2%.

This case study shows how the Darvas Box Theory can effectively capture significant market trends, using Blue Dart Express Ltd. as an example. By methodically identifying and trading breakouts above key Ceilings while respecting Floors as stop-loss levels, you can participate in sustained uptrends with a disciplined approach. The 78.2% gain achieved in this trade is a testament to the strength of the Darvas Box strategy when applied with patience, precision, and adherence to the rules of the system. Each breakout was validated by strong volume, confirming the uptrend and allowing the trader to stay in the trade for nearly a year, maximizing the potential of the bullish move.

Summary of Trade

Box No.	Ceiling (Price)	Floor (Price)	Ceiling Formation Date	Floor Formation Date	Breakout Date	Breakout Price	Days to form Box
1	3994	3680	November 03, 2020	November 05, 2020	November 12, 2020	3994	9
2	4299.8	3709	November 17, 2020	December 22, 2020	January 22, 2021	4299.8	36
3	4470	3820	January 25, 2021	February 01, 2021	February 09, 2021	4470	9
4	4949	4501	February 17, 2021	February 23, 2021	March 08, 2021	4949	19
5	5845	4952	March 31, 2021	April 26, 2021	May 19, 2021	5845	49
6	6177.5	5306.5	May 27, 2021	August 11, 2021	September 03, 2021	6177.5	100
7	6544	6176	September 09, 2021	September 21, 2021	September 30, 2021	6544	9

Case Study: Bharat Heavy Electricals Ltd

In this case study, we will explore how the Darvas Box Theory effectively applied to BHEL, which began its breakout journey in late 2022. Let us take it one step at a time. First, we will look at the initial breakout. Then, we will examine the formation of each Darvas Box. Finally, we will wrap up by summarizing the trade's performance.

The case study begins with a significant 250-day breakout at a price level of 82 on November 25, 2022. This breakout marked a pivotal moment, signaling the start of a potential uptrend as the stock moved above a key resistance level. The breakout was a clear signal for entering the trade, setting the stage for the formation of multiple Darvas Boxes as the stock continued its journey upward.

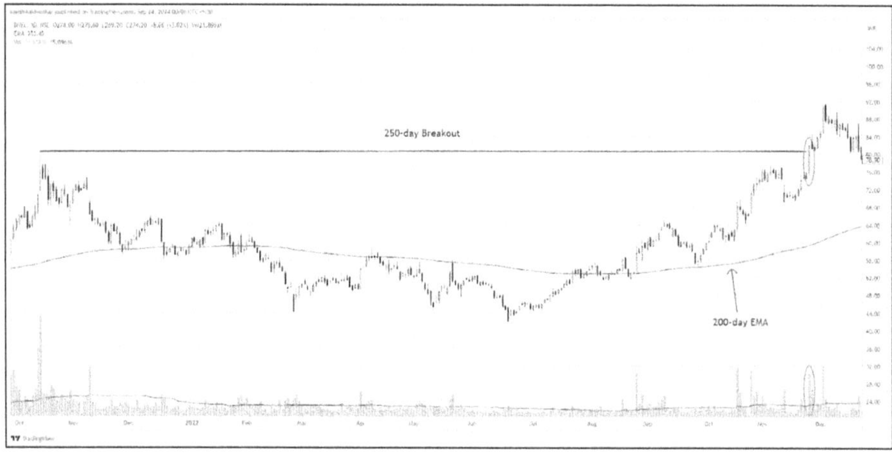

Figure 5.7: Marking of 250-day breakout on daily timeframe Candlestick chart of BHEL

As the stock advanced, it formed a series of Darvas Boxes, each characterized by a Ceiling (resistance level) and a Floor (support level). These boxes provided a structured way to track the stock's progress, with each breakout serving as a confirmation of the ongoing uptrend.

The first Darvas Box formed with a Ceiling at 91.55 on December 05, 2022, and a Floor at 66.30 on February 27, 2023. It took several months for the stock to break out above the Ceiling after consolidating within this range, finally happening on July 05, 2023. The breakout above 91.55 took 130 days from the formation of the Ceiling, and it was accompanied by strong volume, confirming the stock's upward momentum.

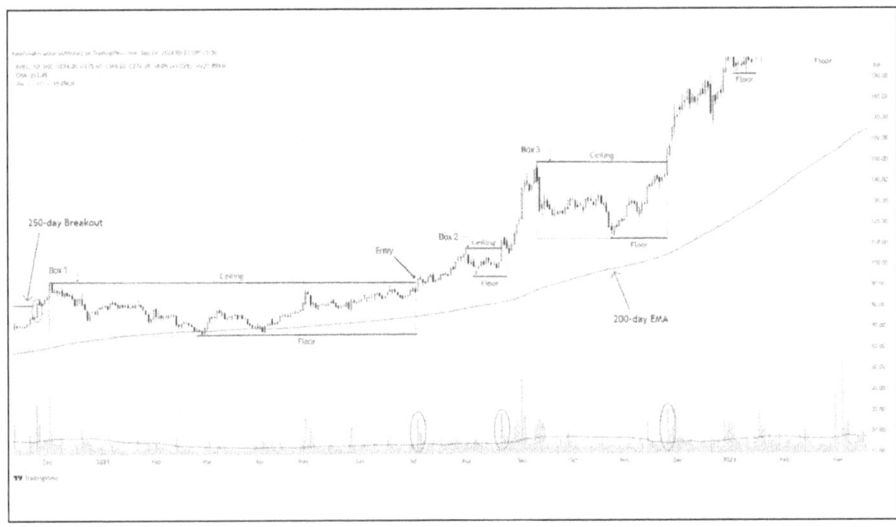

Figure 5.8: Marking of Darvas Box on daily timeframe candlestick chart of BHEL

The second Darvas Box saw a Ceiling at 107.10 on August 01, 2023, and a Floor at 94.80 on August 07, 2023. This time, the stock broke out of the Ceiling relatively quickly, on August 22, 2023, just 21 days after the Ceiling was formed. The quick breakout suggested continued strong bullish momentum, with the volume once again supporting the move.

On September 11, 2023, the third Darvas Box established a Ceiling at 148.90 and a Floor at 113.50 on October 23, 2023. The stock remained in this range for about a month before breaking out above the Ceiling on November 24, 2023.

With a Ceiling at 204.90 on January 02, 2024, and a Floor at 191.85 on January 04, 2024, the fourth Darvas Box was formed. The breakout above the Ceiling occurred on January 17, 2024, just 15 days after the Ceiling was established. The stock continued to show strong momentum, and the breakout was once again supported by significant volume.

The fifth Darvas Box formed with a Ceiling at 275.85 on March 04, 2024, and a Floor at 201.35 on February 13, 2024. The stock broke out above the Ceiling on March 04, 2024, the same day as the Ceiling was formed. This immediate breakout indicated a strong bullish sentiment, with the stock continuing to surge.

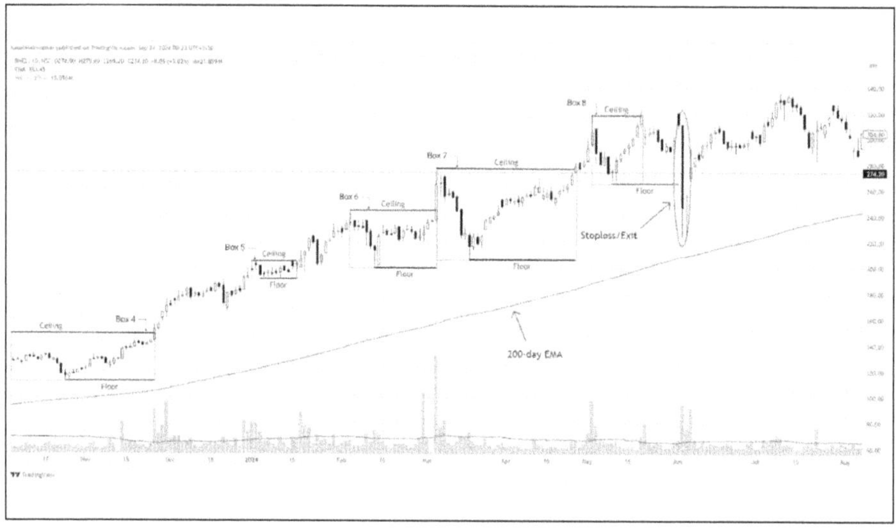

Figure 5.9: Marking of Darvas Box on daily timeframe candlestick chart of BHEL

On March 04, 2024, the sixth Darvas Box had a Ceiling at 275.85 and a Floor at 207.10 on March 15, 2024. The stock broke out above this Ceiling on April 26, 2024, 52 days after the Ceiling was formed. The volume remained strong, confirming the validity of the breakout.

The seventh Darvas Box formed with a Ceiling at 318.30 on May 03, 2024, and a Floor at 267.05 on May 10, 2024. The stock broke out above the Ceiling on May 21, 2024, just 18 days after the Ceiling was established. This was the final breakout before the trend began to lose momentum.

The exit point for this trade was triggered when the price fell below the Floor of the seventh Darvas Box at 267.05 on June 04, 2024. The total trade duration was 192 days, from the initial breakout on November 25, 2022, to the exit on June 04, 2024. During this period, the trade captured a significant move from 82 to 267.05, resulting in a gain of

185.05 points. In percentage terms, the total gain from this trade was approximately 225.7%.

This case study highlights how the Darvas Box Theory can be effectively used to capture substantial gains over an extended period. The 225.7% gain achieved in this trade is a testament to the strength of the Darvas Box strategy. Each breakout was validated by strong volume, confirming the uptrend and allowing the trader to stay in the trade for nearly two years, maximizing the potential of the bullish move.

Summary of Trade

Box No.	Ceiling (Price)	Floor (Price)	Ceiling Formation Date	Floor Formation Date	Breakout Date	Breakout Price	Days to form Box
1	91.55	66.3	December 05, 2022	February 27, 2023	July 05, 2023	91.55	130
2	107.1	94.8	August 01, 2023	August 07, 2023	August 22, 2023	107.1	21
3	148.9	113.5	September 11, 2023	October 23, 2023	November 24, 2023	148.9	44
4	204.9	191.85	January 02, 2024	January 04, 2024	January 17, 2024	204.9	15
5	275.85	201.35	February 05, 2024	February 13, 2024	March 04, 2024	275.85	28
6	275.85	207.1	March 04, 2024	March 15, 2024	April 26, 2024	275.85	52
7	318.3	267.05	May 03, 2024	May 10, 2024	May 21, 2024	318.3	18

Learnings from Nicolas Darvas

Nicolas Darvas, through his trading journey, shared a critical insight that resonates deeply with traders of all levels: he never purchased a stock at its absolute low, nor was he ever able to sell at its absolute high. This acknowledgement highlights the truth that it's important to accept our limitations in trading.

Darvas understood that the essence of successful trading does not lie in precisely timing the market but in adhering to a disciplined system with unwavering commitment. What distinguished him from many traders was his acceptance that he could not capture every single move in the market. He did not strive for the impossible; instead, he focused on executing a system that allowed him to capitalize on the most favorable opportunities.

This philosophy of acceptance is a vital lesson for any trader. It's essential to recognize that we cannot trade every stock, nor can we profit from every market phase. There will always be periods where our strategies may not align perfectly with the prevailing market conditions, and that is perfectly okay. What matters is maintaining discipline and adhering to a tested system, rather than getting caught up in the pursuit of perfection.

By embracing this mindset, you can avoid the emotional pitfalls of fear and greed, which often lead to poor decision-making. Darvas's success was not only because of his technical strategies but also his deep understanding of the market's inherent unpredictability and his steadfast commitment to his trading system.

I am sure that this chapter has provided you with a wealth of insights and a clearer comprehension of the Darvas Box Trading strategy. With this solid foundation, you are better equipped to navigate the complexities of the market and make informed, confident trading decisions. Before we move forward, take a moment to reflect on these lessons and consider how they can be applied to your own trading strategies. With the right mindset and a disciplined approach, you are well on your way to achieving long-term success in trading.

Chapter 6

THE TURTLE TRADING SYSTEM

The Turtle Trading System, developed by Richard Dennis and William Eckhardt, stands as one of the most iconic trend-following systems in trading history. At the first look, it might appear as a refined, more detailed version of the Darvas Box Strategy, with both systems focusing on capturing breakouts. However, the Turtle Trading System goes much deeper, providing clear and rigorous rules for entry, exit, and, most notably, position sizing. This system has had a profound impact on how traders view and manage risk, particularly through its innovative use of the Average True Range (ATR) for determining position size.

When I first delved into the Turtle Trading System, it was the precision and discipline it required that struck me the most. The system's rules for entry and exit were not just about catching breakouts; they were about doing so in a way that consistently managed risk. The methodical approach to position sizing, where positions are calculated based on the ATR and overall capital, introduced me to a level of risk management that was both sophisticated and intuitive.

There is much to learn from this system and the minds of Richard Dennis and William Eckhardt. Their insights into the psychology of trading, the importance of discipline, and the role of a well-structured system continue to resonate deeply with traders around the world. As we delve into this chapter, we will explore how the Turtle Trading System can be applied to modern markets and how its principles can help you become a more disciplined and successful trader.

Introduction to the Turtle Trading Experiment

Have you ever wondered if trading success results from innate talent, or can it actually be taught? In the early 1980s, the two renowned traders, Richard Dennis, and William Eckhardt, put this very question to the test in one of the most intriguing experiments in trading history—the Turtle Trading experiment.

Richard Dennis, known as "The Prince of the Pit," transformed a small loan of $1,600 into more than $200 million by speculating in commodities Futures. Alongside him was his friend and fellow trader, William Eckhardt, a mathematician with a deep interest in the psychology and science of trading. Dennis thought traders could be made, but Eckhardt doubted it. In order to resolve their dispute, they came to an agreement to perform an experiment that would have a lasting impact on the world of trading.

Could Dennis use his trend-following strategy to teach a group of inexperienced individuals to become successful traders? They called their group "The Turtles," a nod to a conversation in which Dennis had suggested that he could grow traders just like turtles were farmed in Singapore. This group included people from various backgrounds—an actor, a security guard, a blackjack player, and even a bartender. Over two weeks of intense training, Dennis taught them a specific set of rules designed to capture long-term trends in the markets. What are the results? Spectacular. The Turtles reportedly made millions in profits, proving Dennis's point: trading could indeed be taught.

The Principles of the Turtle Trading System

The Turtle Trading System is built on the principle of trend following, which is simple yet powerful. According to Dennis and Eckhardt, traders can consistently recognize and leverage the strong trends, either upward or downward, that markets frequently display for financial gain. Instead of predicting the market's direction, Dennis and Eckhardt taught the Turtles to wait for clear signs of a trend and then "ride the wave" as long as possible.

But it was not just about finding trends. Three fundamental principles - discipline, risk management, and consistency - form the basis of the Turtle Trading System.

- **Discipline:** Dennis taught the Turtles to follow strictly the rules he had given them, regardless of their personal beliefs or emotional reactions. It involved adhering to the strategy, even when it felt counterintuitive or uncomfortable. The importance of discipline was evident as the rules aimed to eliminate emotions like fear and greed, common pitfalls for traders.
- **Risk Management:** The Turtle system placed great importance on effectively managing risk. Dennis taught the Turtles to adjust their positions based on market volatility, using a mathematical formula involving the average true range (ATR) of the asset. This prevented them from taking excessive risks on a single trade. Risk management was not just about protecting capital; it was about surviving long enough to capitalize on the big trends.
- **Consistency:** The Turtles also received training to apply the same rules consistently across different markets and timeframes. They traded a wide range of assets, from commodities to currencies, but the rules remained the same. This consistency was key to their success; by following the same strategy repeatedly, they increased their chances of catching and profiting from long-term trends.

Turtle Trading Systems: System 1 and System 2

To implement the trend-following approach, Richard Dennis and William Eckhardt developed two specific trading systems for the Turtles: **System 1** and **System 2**. Both systems were designed to capture trends, but they differed in their entry and exit rules and the timeframe they targeted.

System 1: Short-Term Trend Following

In System 1, the Turtles would initiate a long position (buying) when the price surpassed a 20-day high, signalling a potential upward trend. The long trade would be maintained until the price dipped below the 10-day low, at which point the position would be closed.

For short trades (selling), the strategy was reversed. A short position would be initiated when the price dropped below a 20-day low, indicating a downward trend. This short trade would be squared-off when the price rose above the 10-day high.

An additional rule to prevent over-trading mandated traders to skip the next trade in the same direction if the previous trade was profitable. This rule was designed to avoid engaging in trades during fading trends and to maintain trading discipline.

To manage risk, the turtle initially set a stop-loss at twice the Average True Range (ATR) at the time of the breakout. As the trade progressed, the stop-loss was trailed to the 10-day low for long positions or the 10-day high for short positions. By using an adaptive stop-loss approach, the Turtles were able to make profits and benefit from the trend.

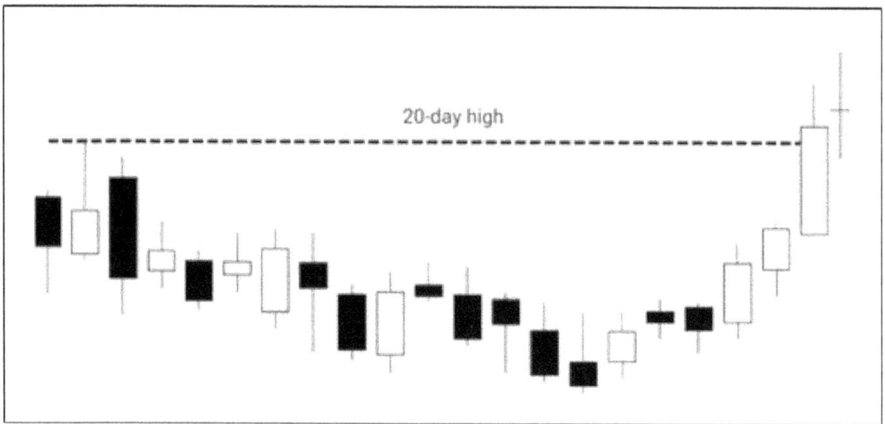

Figure 6.1: Image of System-1

System 2: Long-Term Trend Following

System 2 focused on capturing longer-term trends. In this system, when the price exceeds a 55-day high, signalling a strong upward movement, it initiates a long trade. The position would be held until the price fell below the 20-day low, at which point the trade would be squared-off.

For short trades, the strategy mirrored the approach for long trades but in the opposite direction. The strategy will open a short position when the price falls below a 55-day low, indicating a potential long-term downtrend. The position would be exited when the price rose above the 20-day high.

This system helped the Turtles follow trends over a longer period of time, using specific rules for buying and selling based on price movements.

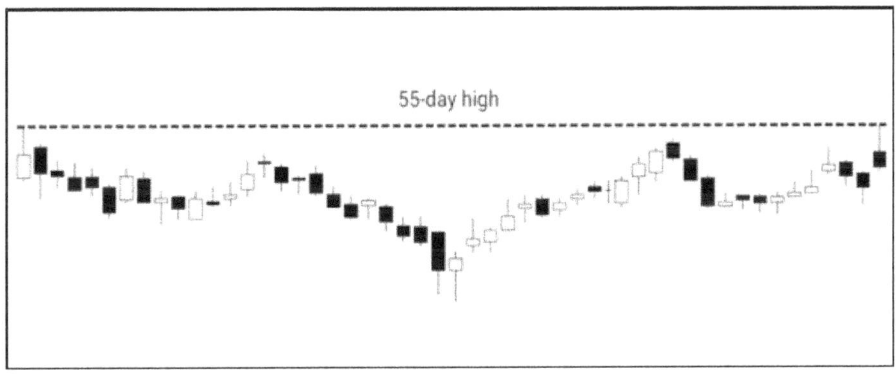

Figure 6.2: Image of System-2

Position Sizing and Pyramiding

One of the most innovative aspects of the Turtle Trading System was its rules for position sizing and pyramiding, which were crucial for managing risk and maximizing returns.

Position Sizing Rules

Richard Dennis and William Eckhardt taught the Turtles to calculate their position sizes based on market volatility, specifically using the

Average True Range (ATR). The key was to ensure that no single trade would risk more than 2% of the total capital. Here's how it worked:

- The maximum stop loss was set to 2 ATR, which meant that each trade had a maximum risk of 2% of the entire capital.
- **Determining the Position Size**: To determine the position size, they calculated the "1 unit" size. For example, if the total capital was 10 lakhs and the ATR was 100 points, the maximum stop loss would be 200 points (2 x ATR = 2 x 100). The maximum risk was set at 2% of capital, or 20,000. Thus, 1 unit would be calculated as 20,000/200 = 100 shares. This calculation ensured that the Turtles were trading a position size that matched the risk level they were willing to accept.

Rules for Pyramiding

Pyramiding, or adding to winning positions, was another key component of the Turtle strategy. The Turtles were instructed to increase their position as the trade moved in their favour, maximizing their exposure to winning trades while still managing risk.

- **Adding Units**: 1 unit would be added at every 0.5 ATR move in favour of the trade. For example, if the ATR was 100 points, an additional unit would be added after every 50-point move in the direction of the trade.
- To ensure risk management and protect profits, the stop loss for all quantities would be set 2 ATR away from the most recent entry point.

The rules helped the Turtles take advantage of strong trends by increasing their positions and also protected them from big losses if the market changed.

Rules of Turtle Trading System 1 and System 2

Rule	System 1: Short-Term Trend Following	System 2: Long-Term Trend Following
Long Entry	Breach of 20-day high price	Breach of 55-day high price
Long Exit	Breach of 10-day low price	Breach of 20-day low price
Short Entry	Breach of 20-day low price	Breach of 55-day low price
Short Exit	Breach of 10-day high price	Breach of 20-day high price
Stop Loss	2 ATR at the time of breakout, then trailed to 10-day low (long) or high (short)	2 ATR at the time of breakout, then trailed to 20-day low (long) or high (short)
Position Sizing	Maximum stop loss of 2% of total capital, quantity determined after calculating 1 unit	Maximum stop loss of 2% of total capital, quantity determined after calculating 1 unit
Pyramiding	Add 1 unit at every 0.5 ATR move in favour of trade	Add 1 unit at every 0.5 ATR move in favour of trade
Pyramiding Stop Loss	2 ATR away from the most recent entry point	2 ATR away from the most recent entry point
Additional Rule	If the previous trade was successful, refrain from taking a new trade in the same direction.	N/A

Case Study: Nifty 50

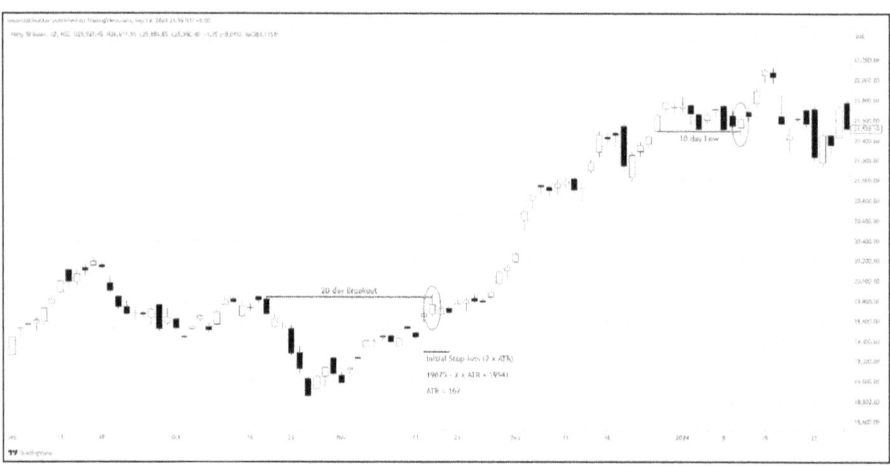

Figure 6.3: Daily timeframe candlestick chart of Nifty explaining System-1

On November 16, 2023, the NIFTY 50 index presented a clear trading opportunity under System 1 of the Turtle Trading Strategy. The trade was initiated when the index broke through its 20-day high, triggering a long entry at 19,875. This breakout suggested a strong upward trend, signalling a good entry point for traders following the system.

According to the Turtle Trading rules, the initial stop-loss was calculated using the Average True Range (ATR) to account for market volatility. With the ATR at 167 points, the stop-loss was set at 19,293, which is 2 times the ATR subtracted from the entry price (19,875 - 2 x 167 = 19,541). This provided a buffer against market fluctuations while still protecting against major losses.

The trade advanced as the NIFTY 50 continued its upward movement. The Turtle Trading System's exit rule for System 1 required holding the position until the price fell below the 10-day low, ensuring that traders could maximize their profits from the ongoing trend. This exit trigger was met on January 10, 2024, when the NIFTY 50 dropped to a 10-day low of 21,490, signalling the time to square-off the trade.

In summary, the trade lasted from November 16, 2023, to January 10, 2024, starting with an entry at 19,875 and closing at 21,490. The calculated stop-loss was effective in protecting the position, and the outcome was a gain of 1,615 points. This concise application of the Turtle Trading System 1 exemplifies how disciplined trading and adherence to systematic rules can lead to successful outcomes in the markets.

Trade Summary

Trade Detail	Value
Entry Date	November 16, 2023
Entry Trigger	Breakout above 20-day high
Entry Price	19,875
ATR Value	167
Initial Stop-Loss	19,541
Exit Date	January 10, 2024
Exit Trigger	Breach of 10-day low
Exit Price	21,490
Total Points Gained	1,615

Case Study: Maruti Suzuki India Ltd (MARUTI)

Let us dive into the case study for System-2 of the Turtle Trading System using MARUTI as our stock of focus.

The trade was initiated on February 24, 2024, when MARUTI's price breached the 55-day high, a key signal in the Turtle Trading System's System-2 strategy. At the time of entry, the stock was trading at 10,973. With an ATR (Average True Range) of 223.63, the initial stop-loss was calculated to manage the risk associated with the trade.

The initial stop-loss was set at 2 times the ATR below the entry price. This resulted in a stop-loss level at 10,525.74, calculated as follows:

Stop-Loss Calculation:

Entry Price - (2 x ATR) = 10,973 - (2 x 223.63) = 10,973 - 447.26 = 10,525.74

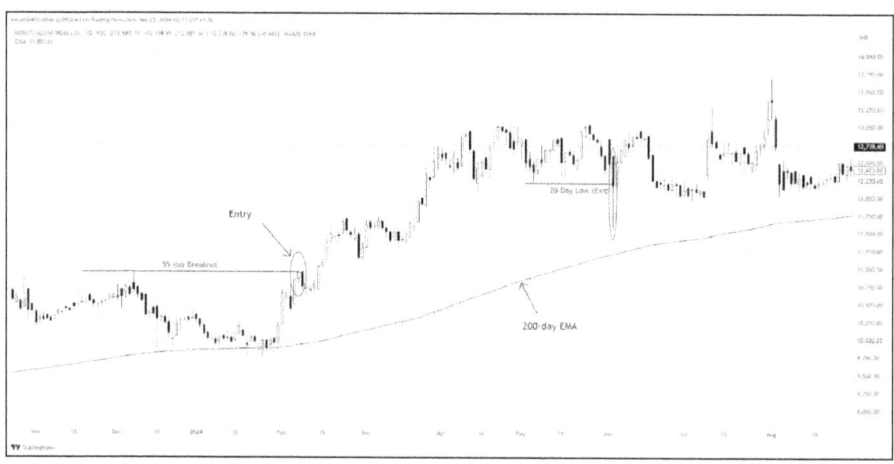

Figure 6.4: Daily timeframe candlestick chart of MARUTI explaining System-1

As the trade progressed, MARUTI continued its upward movement, confirming the strength of the trend. The exit was eventually triggered on June 04, 2024, when the price fell below the 20-day low, which marked the signal to exit the position. The exit was executed at 12,239. Capturing a move of 1266 points.

Throughout the trade, MARUTI traded above its 200-day EMA, further reinforcing the bullish sentiment. While the 200-day EMA is not a part of the traditional Turtle Trading System, it's worth noting from experience that stocks trading above this key moving average often have a higher probability of success. Incorporating such a filter alongside the Turtle rules can enhance the chances of capturing winning trades.

Trade Summary

Trade Detail	Value
Entry Date	February 24, 2024
Entry Trigger	Breakout above 55-day high
Entry Price	10,973
ATR Value	223.63
Initial Stop-Loss	10,525.74
Exit Date	June 04, 2024
Exit Trigger	Breach of 20-day low
Exit Price	12,239
Total Points Gained	1,266

Case Study: Oracle Financial Services Software (OFSS)

Let's walk through the case study for System-2 of the Turtle Trading System using OFSS (Oracle Financial Services Software) as our stock example.

The trade began on December 15, 2023, when OFSS broke above its 55-day high, which is the key entry signal for System-2 in the Turtle Trading strategy. At this point, the stock was trading at 4,253.85. The ATR (Average True Range) at the time of entry was 108.57, which played a crucial role in determining the initial stop-loss to manage the risk associated with this trade.

The initial stop-loss was calculated as 2 times the ATR below the entry price, giving us a stop-loss level at 4,036.71. Here's the calculation:

Stop-Loss Calculation:

Entry Price - (2 x ATR) = 4,253.85 - (2 x 108.57) = 4,253.85 - 217.14 = 4,036.71

Figure 6.5: Daily timeframe candlestick chart of Nifty explaining System-1

As the trade unfolded, OFSS showed strong momentum, continuing to move higher over the following months. The position remained open until April 16, 2024, when the stock's price dropped below the 20-day low, which was the predefined exit trigger. The trade was closed at 7,905. Capturing 3651 points in this trade.

Trade Summary

Trade Detail	Value
Entry Date	December 15, 2023
Entry Trigger	Breakout above 55-day high
Entry Price	4,253.85
ATR Value	108.57
Initial Stop-Loss	4,036.71
Exit Date	April 16, 2024
Exit Trigger	Breach of 20-day low
Exit Price	7,905
Total Points Gained	3,651.15

Learnings from Richard Dennis and William Eckhardt

Exploring the Turtle Trading System reveals its groundbreaking rules, which were ahead of their time. Not many people widely adopted the highly advanced concepts of the system, such as volatility-based stop losses and position sizing, which were integral to it. However, the true genius of the Turtle Trading System was not just in these rules—it lay in the psychology that underpinned them.

Richard Dennis and William Eckhardt understood that the emotions like fear and greed could easily derail even the most well-conceived trading plans. To address this, they created the Turtle rules that reduce emotional influence, enabling traders to follow a structured trading approach. This approach required immense discipline and self-control, especially during periods of market volatility or when trades went against the trader's expectations.

For the Turtles, success was not measured solely by the amount of money made on a single trade; rather, it was gauged by their ability to stick to the rules consistently. In this system, failing to make a trade or deviating from the established rules was considered a failure, regardless of the trade's financial outcome. The emphasis was placed on the process over profits, discipline over discretion, and consistency over quick wins.

One of the most critical aspects of the Turtle Trading System was its emphasis on using stops to avoid large losses. The adage, "There are old traders, and there are bold traders, but there are no old bold traders," aptly applies here. Traders who fail to use stops ultimately risk losing their capital. The Turtles were well aware of this and always implemented stops to protect their equity.

For many, it's far easier to cling to a losing trade, hoping for a turnaround, than to admit defeat and exit the position. However, cutting losses quickly is essential for long-term success. Throughout history, many traders and financial institutions have suffered huge losses because they did not exit losing trades on time.

The most important part of cutting losses is having a predefined exit point before entering a trade. If the market moves against your position, you must exit—no exceptions. This level of discipline differentiates successful traders from those who suffer significant losses.

The Turtles also employed breakout-based exits for profitable positions, a strategy that might seem counterintuitive to many traders. One of the most common mistakes in trend-following systems is exiting a winning position too early. To fully capture a trend, it's important to understand that prices rarely move in a straight line; this often results in temporary declines in profits.

For example, early in a trend, a 10% to 30% profit might evaporate into a small loss due to market fluctuations. Similarly, in the middle of a trend, a substantial 80% to 100% profit might drop by 30% to 40%. The temptation to "lock in profits" is strong, but doing so prematurely can severely limit your overall returns.

The success of the Turtle System relied on allowing winning positions to grow, even if it meant watching significant profits temporarily diminish. The system's exits were designed to capture the full extent of a trend, not just the initial surge. For System 1, the exit was triggered by a 10-day low for long positions or a 10-day high for short positions. System 2 used a 20-day low or high as the exit point. If the price moved against the position by these defined levels, all units in the position were exited.

These exits were some of the most challenging aspects of the Turtle System. It required immense discipline to watch potentially large profits shrink, knowing that holding the position could lead to even greater gains in the long run. This level of discipline is a hallmark of experienced and successful traders.

Even though the Turtle Trading System's rules are simple, they still require a lot of consistency and discipline. Richard Dennis once remarked, "I always say that you could publish my trading rules in the newspaper and no one would follow them. The key is consistency and discipline." This sentiment reflects the reality that while many can create a set of trading rules, few have the confidence and discipline to adhere to them, especially in challenging market conditions.

The performance of the Turtles themselves underscores this point. Despite having access to the same set of rules, not all of them were successful. The issue was not with the rules themselves but with the inability of some traders to follow them consistently. The Turtle Trading System relies on capturing relatively infrequent large trends, which means that there can be extended periods of losses or stagnation. During these times, it's easy to doubt the system and stray from the rules.

One of the original Turtles was even dismissed from the program because he doubted the rules and suspected that Richard Dennis was withholding secret information. This trader's inability to follow the rules, driven by doubt and insecurity, ultimately led to his poor performance.

Another common pitfall for traders is the tendency to modify or ignore the rules. Some Turtles, in an effort to reduce risk, added positions more slowly than the rules specified, only to find that this approach increased the likelihood of being stopped out during market retracements. These subtle changes, while seemingly conservative, could have significant impacts on the system's profitability under certain market conditions.

To build the confidence necessary to follow a trading system's rules—whether it's the Turtle System or any other—it is crucial to conduct personal research using historical trading data and charts. It is not enough to rely on others' experiences or research; you need to get directly involved in the research process. By digging into the trades, analyzing daily equity logs, and becoming intimately familiar with the system's behaviour, you can develop the confidence needed to weather losing periods and stick to the rules.

The Turtle Trading System teaches us that trading success is not just about having the right rules; it is about the discipline to follow them consistently. The ability to stay true to your system, even when it is difficult, is what ultimately separates successful traders from the rest. This system remains a powerful example of the importance of discipline, risk management, and a systematic approach to trading. Richard Dennis and William Eckhardt demonstrated that with the right mindset and a well-defined set of rules, even those new to trading could achieve extraordinary success. The principles laid out in the Turtle Trading System continue to offer valuable lessons for traders today, providing a framework for navigating the complexities of the market with both confidence and consistency. Just as the original Turtles did decades ago, modern traders can harness these timeless strategies to pursue long-term success in the markets.

Chapter 7

BEYOND THE CONTRACTION

Let me introduce you to a pattern that goes beyond mere technical setup—it embodies the trading philosophy of one of the most successful traders of our time, Mark Minervini. Renowned for his exceptional skill and rigorous market approach, Minervini did not begin his journey as a market wizard. Like many traders, he started with modest beginnings and, after enduring several early losses in the 1980s, made a crucial decision to return to the basics. He became scientific in his approach, meticulously analyzing what worked and what did not.

In 1997, Minervini entered the U.S. Investing Championship and emerged victorious, posting an astonishing return of 155% on his initial capital—all with minimal risk. His method was not the result of luck or gambling. Instead, it stemmed from a unique and disciplined approach that blends both fundamental and technical analysis—what he famously refers to as the "Techno-Funda" approach. He studied and drew inspiration from trading legends such as Jesse Livermore, Richard Love, Stan Weinstein, and William Jiler, picking the elements that worked best for him and crafting his own rules-based system that any trader can follow.

Minervini's influence has shaped my trading and investing approach to a large extent. His trend framework and selecting fundamentally strong companies through his methods have become the foundation on which I have built my trading and investing models. His influence has encouraged many traders, including myself, to prioritize a process-driven approach to the markets. This approach focuses on discipline, structure, and consistency.

At the core of Minervini's trading strategy lies the Volatility Contraction Pattern (VCP). The VCP helps traders identify stocks that are likely to have big moves by combining growth drivers and technical analysis. It is not just a pattern; it is a powerful tool that enables traders to capitalize on high-potential trading opportunities.

This chapter helps you master the VCP—not only to understand the pattern but also to effectively apply it, enhancing your ability to uncover stocks that are on the verge of significant breakouts. This method teaches you how to combine technical setups with fundamental analysis, like Minervini did successfully.

The 95% Club: A Blueprint for Success

Before Mark Minervini formulated the Volatility Contraction Pattern (VCP), he did what every successful trader should—he studied past winners. By studying successful stocks, Minervini discovered shared characteristics. This set of features became known as the **"95% Club."**

Minervini's meticulous research revealed that high-performing stocks consistently displayed the following characteristics:

- **99% of these stocks were trading above their 200-day Exponential Moving Average (EMA):** This shows a long-term uptrend, a sign of continued strength.
- **95% were above their 50-day EMA:** This short-term EMA confirms the stock is also strong in the intermediate-term, reinforcing its momentum.
- **95% had a small free float in the market:** Stocks with a small supply see bigger price movements when demand increases. The limited availability of shares can lead to sharp upward moves when institutional buyers come in.
- **95% had shown net profit growth year-over-year (Y-o-Y) or quarter-over-quarter (Q-o-Q):** Profit growth is a fundamental driver for stock price appreciation, as it shows that the company's business is expanding.

- **96% had recently broken out of consolidation or had entered an uptrend:** Stocks poised for strong upward moves often show this technical pattern, where prices tighten before a breakout.
- **95% had a catalyst:** A significant event such as a new product launch, a change in management, or positive earnings often acts as the fuel that propels a stock higher.
- **70% reported more than a 20% increase in earnings in the most recent quarter:** This rapid earnings growth is a hallmark of companies with strong momentum, attracting investors seeking high-growth opportunities.
- **80% had their IPO within the past 10 years:** Newer companies often have more room for growth and are more agile, allowing them to outperform more established firms.

These statistics were not a random collection of data points—they represented a blueprint for stock selection. Minervini understood that almost every big stock winner had these traits in common. They became his first filter for identifying potential candidates for his VCP setup. By focusing on these high-potential stocks, Minervini could develop a strategy that systematically found stocks poised for explosive growth.

The 95% Club offers traders a checklist for identifying stocks that are likely to outperform the market. By applying these filters, traders can significantly narrow their search to focus on high-probability trades that fit the VCP framework.

Minervini's disciplined stock selection method is the foundation of his success and a powerful tool for traders looking for steady high-performance returns.

Trend Framework

To identify and invest in "95% Club" stocks currently in a growth phase, Minervini developed a framework known as the "Trend Framework". This approach helps spot stocks on the brink of significant moves. Minervini crafted a model to identify stocks entering Stage 2: Growth

(Advancing) in their trend. Here are the criteria a stock must meet to qualify:

1. **The price should be trading above its 150-day and 200-day EMA**

    This ensures the stock is in an overall uptrend.

2. **The 150-day EMA must be above the 200-day EMA**

    This adds another layer of confirmation that the trend is strong.

3. **The stock's 50-day EMA must be above the 150-day and 200-day EMA**

    The stock is showing short-term strength, moving above its key moving averages.

4. **The price should be at least 25% above its 52-week low**

    This prevents buying stocks that are still in deep downtrends.

5. **The 200-day EMA should be upward sloping for at least one month (4-5 months preferred)**

    This shows the long-term trend is firmly established.

6. **The current stock price should be within 25% of its 52-week high**

    You want to buy strength, not weakness, and stocks near their highs often have the momentum to keep going.

7. **The stock must be outperforming the Nifty 50 index**

    A rising tide lifts all boats, but you want the strongest boat. The stock should show relative strength. *To make this objective, use the stock's relative strength ratio chart and ensure its 30 EMA is above its 60 EMA.*

8. **The current market price should be above the 50-day EMA**

    The stock is in an immediate uptrend.

And there's more. Before a stock meets these conditions, it must also have improved earnings or sales, Y-o-Y or at least Q-o-Q. This fundamental growth serves as the foundation for the technical strength we see on the charts.

These rules provide a clear roadmap to find stocks that are entering a Growth stage. Once you have identified a stock that meets these criteria, it is time to look for the VCP pattern.

Recognizing the VCP Patterns

Once we have filtered for strong fundamentals and technical setups, we can delve into the Volatility Contraction Pattern (VCP). The VCP is about the tightening of price action, signalling that a stock is building up momentum for a breakout. Think of it like a spring being compressed: the more tightly it coils, the more energy it stores for the eventual breakout.

The VCP is a powerful pattern because it reveals the psychology of the market. The price action reflects the interaction between buyers and sellers, with sellers slowly losing their grip and buyers stepping in with increasing confidence. This is where volatility contraction comes into play, giving traders a visual cue that the stock is preparing for a move.

Here is how you can recognize and understand the key characteristics of a VCP:

Price Contraction

The initial and most important attribute of a VCP is price contraction. This is the defining characteristic of the pattern, happening when the stock's price narrows its range. The size of each pullback decreases compared to the one before. For example, the first pullback might be 15%, the second 10%, and the third 5%. The decrease in price movement shows that people are selling less and buying more.

You will witness a series of downward moves where the stock initially has wide swings, but over time, these swings get smaller, demonstrating that volatility is decreasing. This compression is a key sign that the stock is preparing for a breakout. The volatility contraction acts like a pressure cooker, where market participants are waiting for the right moment to either push the price up or down. In most cases, this contraction leads to a bullish breakout as buyers overpower sellers.

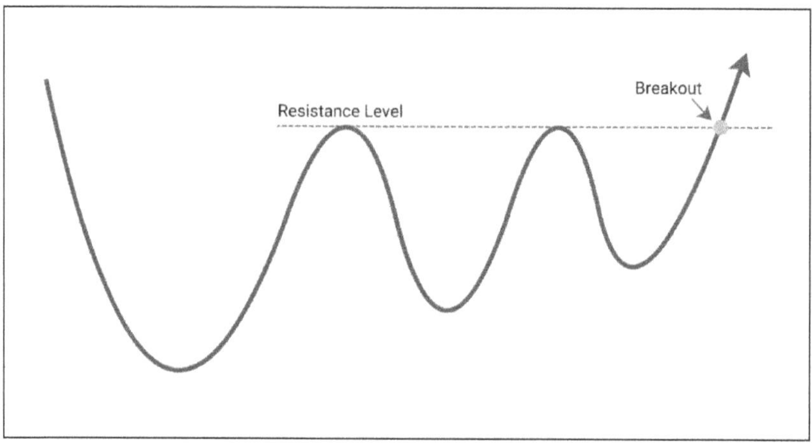

Figure 7.1: Image of Price Contraction

Higher Lows or Equal Bottoms

The second important characteristic to watch for in a VCP pattern is higher-lows or equal bottoms. In a healthy VCP setup, each time the stock pulls back, it either forms a higher-low, or the stock finds support at the same level, creating equal bottoms.

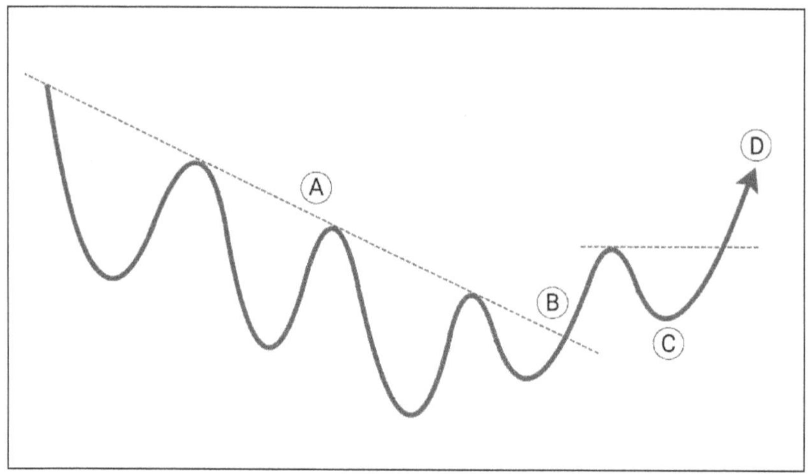

Figure 7.2: Image of Higher-lows of Equal Bottoms

When a stock forms higher-lows, it is a signal that strong hands (institutional buyers or savvy investors) are accumulating the stock, stepping in earlier with each dip and pushing the price higher. Higher-lows are one of the most encouraging signals within a VCP because they show increasing demand at progressively higher price points. Even when sellers push the price down, the buyers step in sooner than before, keeping the price from falling as far as it did during previous pullbacks.

There are instances where you may notice equal bottoms rather than higher-lows. This indicates that the stock is finding solid support at a certain level, but the point is the same: there is a strong demand that keeps the price from falling further.

Resistance and Support Dynamics

The third key feature of the VCP is the interaction between resistance and support. The price contraction causes the pattern's top to become a resistance level, resulting in sellers persistently resisting any upward price movements. However, the bottoms of the pattern act as support, with buyers stepping in to prevent the price from dropping below a certain level.

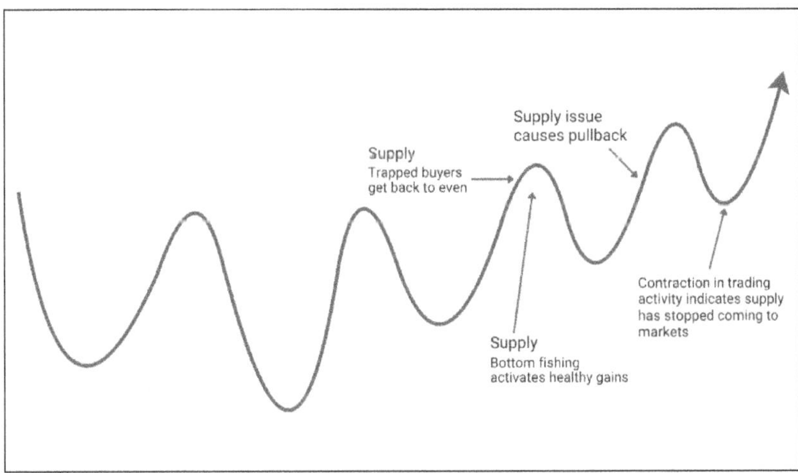

Figure 7.3: Image of Resistance and Support Dynamics

This dynamic creates a tug-of-war between buyers and sellers. The stock's price narrows in a tight range as both sides become more cautious. This tight consolidation makes the VCP so effective. The longer this fight goes on, the bigger the breakthrough will be.

Often, the stock will test the resistance level multiple times but struggle to break through until there is enough momentum. As the resistance level is tested more times, the stock becomes more likely to breakout once the sellers have been exhausted.

VCP in Different Patterns

It is important to note that the VCP does not limit itself to one specific shape or form. Instead, it can manifest in several classic chart patterns:

1. **Cup and Handle**: In this pattern, the "cup" forms as the stock pulls back and consolidates, followed by a smaller pullback, or "handle," before the breakout. The contraction happens as the price pulls back less with each drop.

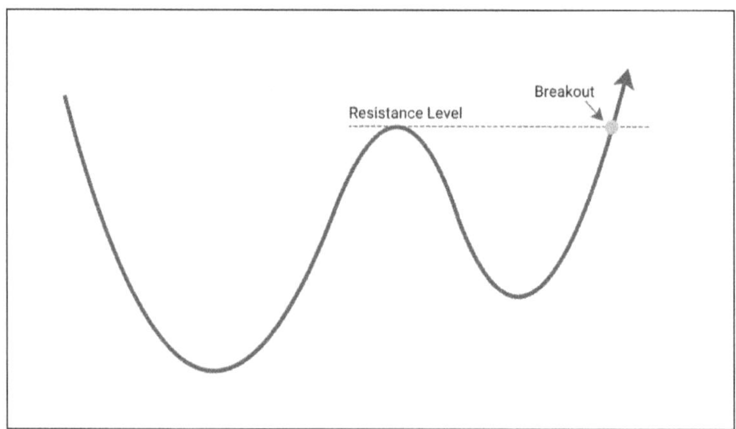

Figure 7.4: Image of Cup & Handle

2. **Cup with Multiple Handles**: Similar to the Cup and Handle, but with additional consolidation phases, where each "handle" forms a smaller and tighter range than the last.

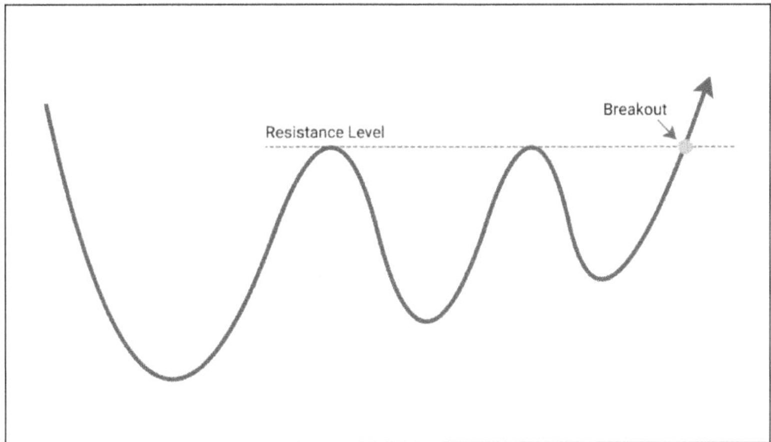

Figure 7.5: Image of Cup with Multiple Handles

3. **Rectangle Patterns**: In this variation, the price oscillates between horizontal support and resistance levels, forming a tight rectangular trading range. The contractions happen as the price makes smaller moves within the rectangle.

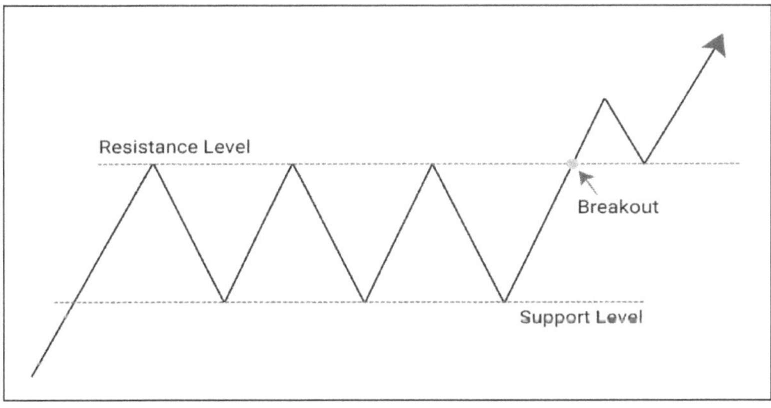

Figure 7.6: Image of Cup with Multiple Handles

4. **Ascending Triangle**: This is a bullish pattern where the price forms higher-lows while resistance stays flat. The VCP manifests as the price contracting into the point of the triangle, which leads to a breakout.

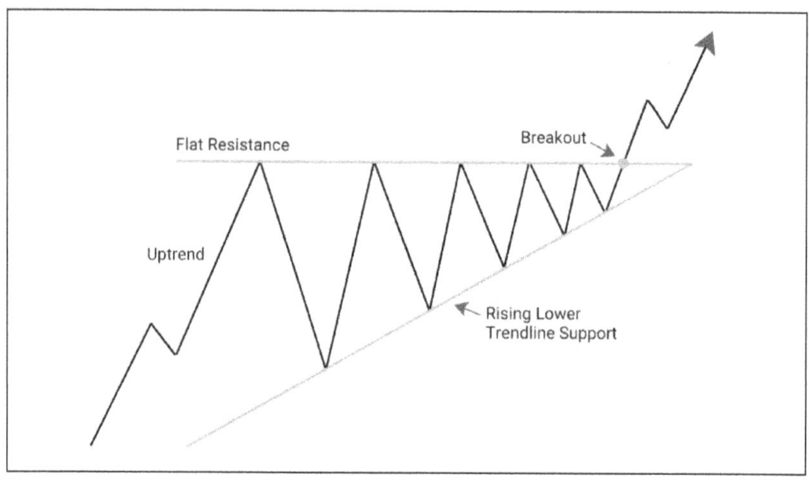

Figure 7.7: Image of Ascending Triangle

Across all these patterns, the fundamental concept remains the same - volatility contracts, and the price tightens up like a spring, getting ready for a breakout. Each of these patterns indicates that the buyers are stepping in, selling pressure is weakening, and the stock is getting ready for a significant move.

VCP is more than a typical technical pattern. It is a reflection of market psychology, showing you when the balance of power is shifting from sellers to buyers. By understanding how price contraction, higher-lows or equal bottoms, and resistance and support dynamics work together, you will be able to spot this powerful pattern and position yourself to capture explosive moves when the breakout finally happens.

VCP patterns are about patience and discipline. As volatility contracts, it signals that the stock is preparing for a breakout. By identifying and acting on this pattern, you can take advantage of significant price moves with minimized risk. The VCP helps traders focus on high-probability setups, positioning them to enter at the most opportune moment, right before the stock makes its big move.

How to Trade the VCP: Entry and Exit Strategies

Recognizing the Volatility Contraction Pattern (VCP) is just the first step. Knowing how to trade it, when to enter the position, and when to exit is crucial for capitalizing on the pattern's potential. Here, I will break down entry and exit strategies so you can execute trades with confidence.

Entry Strategy

The success of any trade depends largely on timing. With the VCP, your goal is to enter at the precise moment when the stock is about to break from its final contraction phase, indicating that it is ready for a significant move.

1. Wait for the Breakout

The most critical rule for entering a VCP trade is to wait for the breakout. Avoid entering prematurely, as prices may contract or break down. The ideal entry point occurs when the stock price breaks out above the upper boundary of the final contraction, typically a resistance level formed by the last pullback.

Why is the breakout important? This indicates that there is more demand than supply. The shrinking volatility in the stock price—evidenced by smaller and smaller contractions—tells us that sellers are stepping aside, and buyers are becoming more aggressive. When the price finally breaches the resistance level, it is a clear sign that the buyers have won the tug-of-war, and the stock is ready to move upwards.

But a breakout alone is not enough. You want to see a confirmation of the breakout with a noticeable increase in volume. A volume surge at the breakout point is a key indicator of strong buying interest, and it validates that the breakout is real, not a false move.

2. Use a Buy-Stop Order

To optimize your entry strategy, consider using a buy-stop order. A buy-stop order allows you to enter the trade automatically once the stock reaches a specific price, typically just above the resistance level. This ensures that you are not entering too early and only participate if the stock breaks out as expected.

For instance, if the upper boundary of the VCP is at 100, you will set your buy-stop order slightly above, at 101. If the stock hits 101, it will trigger your buy order, confirming that the breakout has occurred and that you are now in the trade.

This tactic is especially useful for traders who cannot monitor the market constantly. Furthermore, it reduces the emotional stress of manually timing your entry, ensuring adherence to the plan and confirmation of the market's movement.

Exit Strategy

Knowing when to exit is equally important as knowing when to enter the trade. The key to a successful exit strategy is managing your risk while maximizing your gains.

1. Initial Stop Loss

Every good trade starts with a solid risk management plan. After entering a position, set an initial stop loss just below the low of the final contraction in the VCP pattern. This protects you if the breakout fails and the stock reverses.

For instance, if the final pullback low was at 95, place your stop loss at 94. If the price drops below this, you are automatically out of the trade, limiting your loss.

2. Trailing Stop

As the trade moves in your favour, use a trailing stop to protect your gains while allowing the trade to grow. A trailing stop adjusts upward as the stock price rises, ensuring profits are captured if the stock reverses. For instance, after a significant price move, raise your stop loss to just below the latest swing low. This locks in profits if the stock declines. Give the stock space to fluctuate without premature exits. Adjust your trailing stop based on the stock's price action and volatility to maximize potential gains.

Case Study: Amber Enterprises India Ltd (AMBER)

In this case study, we will explore how Amber Enterprises India Ltd., a prominent manufacturer of air conditioners and components, aligns with the Volatility Contraction Pattern (VCP) and Specific Entry Point Analysis (SEPA) framework developed by Mark Minervini. This will help us gain practical insights into the application of Minervini's model, not just in theory, but through real-world stock analysis.

We will use Minervini's model to analyze both Amber's fundamental and technical data. This model focuses on fundamentals, technical analysis, and the Volatility Contraction Pattern (VCP).

Years											TTM
Sales (Revenue)	1,230.27	1,089.03	1,661.50	2,320.06	2,781.99	3,962.79	3,030.52	4,206.40	6,927.10	6,729.21	7,429.00
Cost of Goods sold (COGS)	[illegible]	[illegible]	[illegible]	[illegible]	[illegible]	[illegible]	[illegible]	[illegible]	[illegible]	[illegible]	
Gross Profit	[illegible]	[illegible]	[illegible]	[illegible]	[illegible]	[illegible]	[illegible]	[illegible]	[illegible]	[illegible]	
Gross Profit Margin (GPM)	[illegible]	[illegible]	[illegible]	[illegible]	[illegible]	[illegible]	[illegible]	[illegible]	[illegible]	[illegible]	
Total Expense	[illegible]	[illegible]	[illegible]	[illegible]	[illegible]	[illegible]	[illegible]	[illegible]	[illegible]	[illegible]	[illegible]
EBITDA (Operating Profit)	[illegible]	[illegible]	[illegible]	[illegible]	[illegible]	[illegible]	[illegible]	[illegible]	[illegible]	[illegible]	[illegible]
EBITDA Margin (OPM %)	[illegible]	[illegible]	[illegible]	[illegible]	[illegible]	[illegible]	[illegible]	[illegible]	[illegible]	[illegible]	[illegible]
Other Income	[illegible]	[illegible]	[illegible]	[illegible]	[illegible]	[illegible]	[illegible]	[illegible]	[illegible]	[illegible]	[illegible]
Depreciation	[illegible]	[illegible]	[illegible]	[illegible]	[illegible]	[illegible]	[illegible]	[illegible]	[illegible]	[illegible]	[illegible]
EBIT	[illegible]	[illegible]	[illegible]	[illegible]	[illegible]	[illegible]	[illegible]	[illegible]	[illegible]	[illegible]	[illegible]
EBIT %	[illegible]	[illegible]	[illegible]	[illegible]	[illegible]	[illegible]	[illegible]	[illegible]	[illegible]	[illegible]	[illegible]
Interest	[illegible]	[illegible]	[illegible]	[illegible]	[illegible]	[illegible]	[illegible]	[illegible]	[illegible]	[illegible]	[illegible]
Profit Bef. Exceptional Item	[illegible]	[illegible]	[illegible]	[illegible]	[illegible]	[illegible]	[illegible]	[illegible]	[illegible]	[illegible]	
Exceptional Item											[illegible]
Profit Before tax (EBT)	[illegible]	[illegible]	[illegible]	[illegible]	[illegible]	[illegible]	[illegible]	[illegible]	[illegible]	[illegible]	[illegible]
Tax Paid	[illegible]	[illegible]	[illegible]	[illegible]	[illegible]	[illegible]	[illegible]	[illegible]	[illegible]	[illegible]	[illegible]
Tax Rate %	[illegible]	[illegible]	[illegible]	[illegible]	[illegible]	[illegible]	[illegible]	[illegible]	[illegible]	[illegible]	
Net Profit (PAT)	[illegible]	[illegible]	[illegible]	[illegible]	[illegible]	[illegible]	[illegible]	[illegible]	[illegible]	[illegible]	[illegible]
PAT Margin (NPM %)	[illegible]	[illegible]	[illegible]	[illegible]	[illegible]	[illegible]	[illegible]	[illegible]	[illegible]	[illegible]	[illegible]
Earnings Per Share (EPS)	[illegible]	[illegible]	[illegible]	[illegible]	[illegible]	[illegible]	[illegible]	[illegible]	[illegible]	[illegible]	[illegible]
Dividend Payout Ratio %		[illegible]				[illegible]					

Figure 7.8: P&L Statement of AMBER from FY 2014 to FY 2024

Amber Enterprises India Ltd. has shown robust growth in both its fundamentals and technical performance, making it a compelling case study to apply Mark Minervini's model. The company has shown consistent revenue and earnings growth over the years, with its sales rising from ₹1,230 crores in FY 2015 to ₹6,729 crores in FY 2024 (March). The company's profits have gone up due to the increase in sales. Net profit grew from ₹28.77 crores to ₹176 crores in the same period. Amber's Earnings Per Share (EPS) also reflects this positive trajectory, increasing from ₹13.26 in FY 2015 to ₹32.41 in FY 2024, indicating a growing return for the shareholders. These indicators match Minervini's strategy of choosing stocks with high earnings growth and increasing profit margins.

Figure 7.9: Daily timeframe Candlestick chart of AMBER along with 50-period, 150-period, and 200-period EMA

In Amber Enterprises, you can see a classic example of the Volatility Contraction Pattern (VCP), which is a fundamental aspect of Minervini's methodology. Based on Minervini's analysis, the stock is showing strong technical performance by trading above key moving averages of 50, 150, and 200-day EMA. The price chart shows multiple periods of price contraction, with the stock forming narrower price ranges, suggesting reduced volatility and increased accumulation by institutional investors. These periods of tightening are often followed by breakouts, which are supported by significant volume spikes, further validating the price movement. This price action suggests that Amber is coiling up for a breakout, a key signal that Minervini looks for in his VCP pattern analysis.

Amber Enterprises India Ltd. presents a strong case of aligning both its fundamental performance and technical setup. By balancing its earnings growth, price contraction patterns, and risk management strategies, AMBER demonstrates how Minervini's model can be effectively applied to identify stocks that are poised for significant moves, offering traders an opportunity to enter trades with precision and manage risk effectively.

Case Study: Bharti Airtel Ltd.

Bharti Airtel Ltd. demonstrated consistent growth both in revenue and market share. Its price action and technical patterns align well with the principles developed by Mark Minervini. In this case study, we will analyze Bharti Airtel's performance through the lens of the principles laid down, looking at key components such as earnings growth, relative strength, and volatility contraction patterns (VCP) for identifying high-potential entry and exit points.

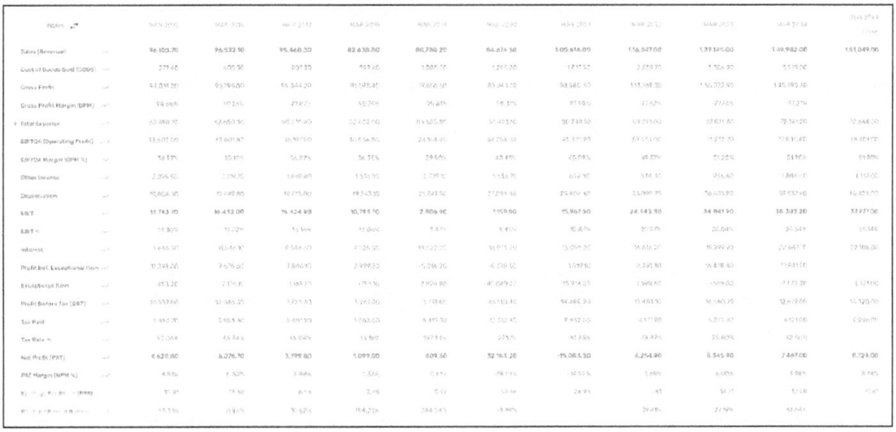

Years	MAR 2015	MAR 2016	MAR 2017	MAR 2018	MAR 2019	MAR 2020	MAR 2021	MAR 2022	MAR 2023	MAR 2024	JUN 2024 TTM
Sales (Revenue)	96,100.70	96,532.90	95,468.30	82,638.80	80,780.20	84,674.50	1,00,616.09	1,16,547.00	1,39,145.00	1,49,982.00	1,51,049.00
Cost of Goods Sold (COGS)	277.40	[illegible]	997.30	[illegible]	[illegible]	[illegible]	[illegible]	[illegible]	[illegible]	[illegible]	
Gross Profit	[illegible]	[illegible]	[illegible]	[illegible]	[illegible]	[illegible]	[illegible]	[illegible]	[illegible]	[illegible]	
Gross Profit Margin (GPM)	[illegible]	[illegible]	[illegible]	[illegible]	[illegible]	[illegible]	[illegible]	[illegible]	[illegible]	[illegible]	
Total Expense	[illegible]	[illegible]	[illegible]	[illegible]	[illegible]	[illegible]	[illegible]	[illegible]	[illegible]	[illegible]	[illegible]
EBITDA (Operating Profit)	33,607.00	[illegible]	[illegible]	[illegible]	[illegible]	[illegible]	[illegible]	[illegible]	[illegible]	[illegible]	[illegible]
EBITDA Margin (OPM %)	[illegible]	[illegible]	[illegible]	36.36%	[illegible]	[illegible]	[illegible]	[illegible]	[illegible]	[illegible]	[illegible]
Other Income	[illegible]	[illegible]	[illegible]	[illegible]	[illegible]	[illegible]	[illegible]	[illegible]	[illegible]	[illegible]	[illegible]
Depreciation	[illegible]	[illegible]	[illegible]	[illegible]	[illegible]	[illegible]	[illegible]	[illegible]	[illegible]	[illegible]	[illegible]
EBIT	[illegible]	16,432.00	[illegible]	10,796.70	2,806.90	[illegible]	[illegible]	24,143.30	34,841.90	36,343.20	[illegible]
EBIT %	14.30%	[illegible]	[illegible]	[illegible]	[illegible]	[illegible]	[illegible]	20.07%	20.04%	[illegible]	[illegible]
Interest	[illegible]	[illegible]	9,544.00	[illegible]	[illegible]	[illegible]	[illegible]	[illegible]	10,399.20	[illegible]	[illegible]
Profit incl. Exceptional Items	[illegible]	[illegible]	[illegible]	2,999.20	[illegible]	[illegible]	[illegible]	8,345.90	16,438.40	[illegible]	
Exceptional Items	[illegible]	[illegible]	[illegible]	[illegible]	2,926.80	[illegible]	[illegible]	[illegible]	[illegible]	[illegible]	[illegible]
Profit Before Tax (PBT)	[illegible]	[illegible]	[illegible]	[illegible]	[illegible]	[illegible]	[illegible]	[illegible]	[illegible]	[illegible]	[illegible]
Tax Paid	[illegible]	[illegible]	[illegible]	1,082.00	[illegible]	[illegible]	[illegible]	[illegible]	[illegible]	[illegible]	[illegible]
Tax Rate %	[illegible]	[illegible]	[illegible]	[illegible]	[illegible]	[illegible]	[illegible]	[illegible]	[illegible]	[illegible]	[illegible]
Net Profit (PAT)	6,620.80	6,076.70	3,799.80	1,099.00	409.50	32,183.20	-15,083.50	8,254.90	8,345.90	7,467.00	8,724.00
PAT Margin (NPM %)	4.5%	6.52%	3.94%	1.32%	0.51%	[illegible]	[illegible]	[illegible]	6.00%	[illegible]	[illegible]
EPS (Rs)	[illegible]	[illegible]	[illegible]	[illegible]	[illegible]	[illegible]	[illegible]	[illegible]	[illegible]	[illegible]	[illegible]
[illegible]	[illegible]	[illegible]	[illegible]	[illegible]	[illegible]			[illegible]	[illegible]	[illegible]	

Figure 7.10: P&L Statement of BHARTIARTL from FY 2014 to FY 2024

The fundamental analysis reveals that Bharti Airtel has shown robust revenue growth, as seen in its yearly P&L statement. Over the years, the company has maintained a steady upward trend in revenue from 96,100.70 crores in March 2015 to 1,51,049.00 crores in June 2024. Moreover, the company's EBITDA margin has remained strong, hitting

25.14% in June 2024, which shows that they are operating efficiently. Bharti Airtel's strong balance sheet and profitability metrics, such as its 5.87% PAT margin in June 2024, align with Minervini's requirement for selecting fundamentally sound stocks with positive earnings growth.

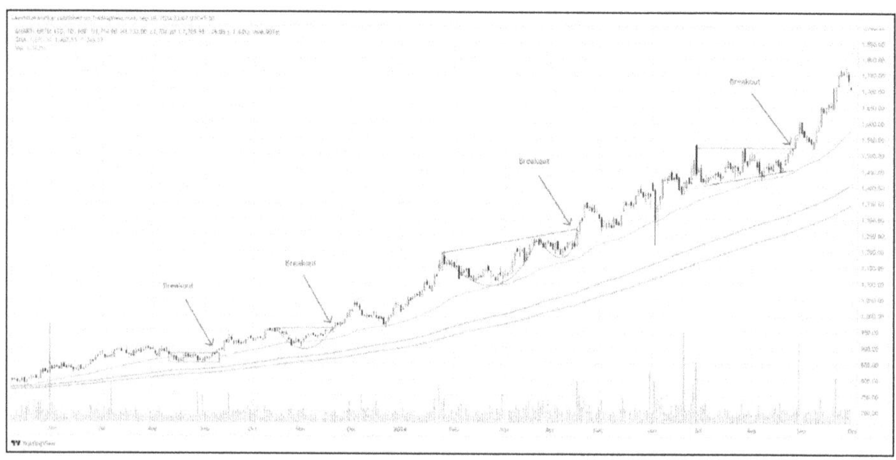

Figure 7.11: Daily timeframe Candlestick chart of BHARTIARTL along with 50-period, 150-period, and 200-period EMA

From a technical standpoint, the provided chart showcases a series of breakouts that align. Notably, Bharti Airtel has consistently respected its 50-day, 150-day, and 200-day exponential moving averages (EMA), which is a hallmark of stocks that exhibit relative strength in the market. Bharti Airtel experienced multiple breakouts in 2024, signifying significant buying pressure as it continued to trade well above its 200-day EMA.

The Volatility Contraction Pattern (VCP) is particularly evident in the stock's movement. Over time, Bharti Airtel has gone through periods of tight consolidation, where price contractions became smaller, indicating that sellers were being absorbed. The price action on the chart shows several pullbacks, followed by breakouts, particularly in August 2024. These smaller contractions, followed by breakouts with higher volumes, signify the buildup of momentum, a key characteristic of the VCP pattern.

Bharti Airtel Ltd. aligns well with the model as outlined by Mark Minervini. It meets the key criteria of having a strong foundation, being technically sound, and employing effective risk management. By following the principles, traders can potentially capitalize on the stock's continued upward momentum.

The Psychology of Trading the VCP

When we consider trading, we often focus on strategies, setups, and technical analysis, but an equally crucial component is often overlooked—trading psychology. In the world of trading, especially with patterns like the Volatility Contraction Pattern (VCP), how you think and react can be just as important as the strategies you employ. Let us dive into the psychological challenges and rewards that come with trading the VCP.

At its core, the VCP is about a series of contractions—moments when the price pulls back and then tightens again. While this may sound straightforward, these pullbacks can be emotionally taxing for traders, especially when they occur several times before a breakout. When you see the stock pull back, fear and doubt may creep in. You might start second-guessing your strategy, asking yourself questions like, "What if this contraction is different?" or "What if the stock crashes instead of breaking out?" This emotional volatility is often harder to manage than price volatility because it tests your ability to stick to a plan.

For new or impatient traders, this is a key psychological challenge. The temptation to jump into the trade too early can be overwhelming, especially when you are eager to see results. You might think, "I'll enter now before the breakout happens," but jumping in prematurely can lead to exposure to further pullbacks or a false breakout. It takes discipline to wait for the right setup to develop. On the other hand, there is the danger of exiting a position too soon. As the stock experiences each contraction, it is easy to get nervous and exit the trade, fearing a larger decline. However, these pullbacks are natural and part of the stock's accumulation process, where strong hands take over from weak hands. Selling too early because of short-term pullbacks can mean missing out on the eventual breakout that the VCP is known for.

If there is one psychological trait that defines successful VCP traders, it is patience. The VCP is not a fast-moving pattern, and it takes time for the stock to go through multiple phases of contraction before it finally breaks out. Waiting for the ideal breakout requires mental stamina. Many traders feel the pressure to act quickly, worried they will miss the move if they wait too long. But in trading, timing is everything. Acting out of impatience can lead to poor decisions, like entering too early or exiting too soon. The VCP teaches traders that the best opportunities come to those who can wait through the uncertainty and trust the process. Patience rewards those who stick to their strategy, recognizing that each contraction brings the stock one step closer to the eventual breakout.

Another psychological challenge in trading the VCP is the need for discipline. When the market moves against you—even temporarily—there is always the temptation to abandon the plan. You might see other stocks moving faster, and the fear of missing out (FOMO) can cloud your judgement, making you question the VCP setup you are following. But discipline is the cornerstone of VCP trading. The VCP is not about reacting to every market twitch; it is about following a structured approach where you trust the setup, not your emotions. The pattern itself helps traders manage risk by showing clear, defined contractions. More contraction equals less volatility, the ideal moment to wait for the breakout.

Sticking to the plan means waiting for all the technical signals to align: narrowing price ranges, higher-lows, shrinking volatility, and a confirmed breakout with volume. Markets can be unpredictable, and not every VCP setup will go as planned. That is why you need the discipline to trust the strategy, wait for the ideal entry point, and use the right risk management techniques, like stop losses.

One of the most common emotions traders face is FOMO—the fear of missing out. In VCP trading, this can be particularly problematic during periods of consolidation or when the stock is just on the verge of a breakout. You may see other traders profiting from fast-moving stocks, or you might feel impatient after waiting through several contractions. This feeling of missing out can lead to rash decisions, such as entering the trade before all the conditions are met. However, jumping in before the breakout materializes can lead to disappointing results, as the stock may still need more time to consolidate. The VCP pattern is a lesson in self-control. You need to remind yourself that it is better to miss an opportunity than to enter a trade without the right signals. FOMO-driven trades often result in bigger losses or missed opportunities when the true breakout finally happens.

The VCP teaches a valuable lesson: uncertainty is part of the game. Traders must accept market uncertainty. No guarantees, even after identifying patterns and waiting for breakouts. However, by trading the VCP, you learn to embrace uncertainty productively. You believe that contracting volatility indicates tightening supply, each pullback represents accumulation, and the eventual breakout is the result of this energy build-up.

This mental shift is crucial. Instead of trying to predict every market move, you start to trust that the setup will eventually pay off, even if the short-term movements are uncomfortable or unclear. The VCP pattern, when traded with patience and discipline, provides a structure that helps traders remain calm in the face of market noise.

Mastering the psychology of trading the VCP is not just about executing a technical strategy—it is about developing the mindset necessary for long-term success in trading. Traders who can remain patient, trust the setup, and follow their plan through multiple contractions are rewarded not only with potential profits but also with the confidence that comes from discipline and control. The VCP is as much a psychological test as it is technical. By learning to embrace pullbacks, wait for the breakout, and manage your emotions, you become a more effective and resilient trader. Over time, this mindset helps you navigate the inevitable ups and downs of the market with greater clarity and focus, making it easier to recognize and seize the big opportunities when they present themselves.

In the end, trading the VCP successfully requires more than just chart reading—it requires mental fortitude. By staying patient, trusting the process, and resisting emotional impulses, you can master the psychological side of trading and enhance your overall performance in the markets.

As we have explored throughout this chapter, the Volatility Contraction Pattern (VCP) is more than just a technical setup—it is a proven strategy that reflects years of market wisdom and discipline, pioneered by Mark Minervini. In the following chapters, we will build on these concepts and integrate them into broader strategies, helping you apply the lessons of the VCP to different market conditions and timeframes. The journey to mastering this pattern begins with understanding, but it is solidified through practice and execution.

Chapter 8

MULTI-TIMEFRAME MOMENTUM TRADING USING POINT & FIGURE (P&F) CHARTS

Trading successfully in the markets requires not just skill but also an edge—something that sets you apart and gives you the confidence to execute your trades with precision. One powerful way to gain that edge is by using multi-timeframe analysis, a technique that allows traders to view market movements across different timeframes to identify the broader trend and the ideal entry and exit points. Over the years, I have found that incorporating multiple timeframes into my trading has been invaluable, particularly when combined with the Point & Figure (P&F) charting method.

I started using P&F charts in 2019, and since then, this charting style has become a cornerstone of my trading and investing approach. Unlike other chart types, P&F charts remove insignificant price movements, reducing the likelihood of hasty decisions or second-guessing. With P&F, I have been able to see the market more clearly, focusing on significant price changes that truly matter.

In this chapter, I want to share a strategy that is deeply inspired by the concept of 'Pattern Cluster,' as documented by Prashant Shah of Definedge. His work in the realm of P&F has profoundly influenced my approach, and I have drawn heavily on his methodologies to develop a trading strategy that is both objective and practical. The strategy we will explore is designed to help you harness the power of P&F charts through a clear, rule-based approach that removes guesswork from your trading.

By the end of this chapter, my goal is to equip you with a well-defined strategy for trading with P&F charts, complete with specific entry and exit rules you can apply to your own trading. It's more than learning a new technique that can give you the clarity and confidence to make more informed trading decisions.

Introduction to P&F Charts

When it comes to analyzing markets, traders often rely on candlesticks or bar charts—charts that move with time. They give you an overview of price action in a specific time frame: daily, weekly, or even minute-by-minute. What if we remove the concept of time and only consider price? That is where Point & Figure (P&F) charts come into play, and this makes these charts so unique.

P&F charts have been around for over a century, and focus only on price movements. Unlike time-based charts that record price changes at regular intervals, P&F charts only mark significant price movements. If the price does not move enough to meet a set threshold (known as the box size), the chart plots nothing, neither a 'X' nor an 'O'. These charts are so simple that they eliminate the noise, allowing for a clear view of trends, breakout levels, and price reversals.

By removing the time element, P&F charts provide a clear and objective view of the market. For momentum traders who want to capitalize on trends and avoid the clutter of short-term fluctuations, P&F charts offer an ideal tool. In this chapter, we will explore how multi-timeframe analysis on P&F charts helps you spot powerful trends, time your entries with precision, and manage your trades.

I understand you will be new to P&F charts, so before we get into the details of multi-timeframe trading with P&F charts, let me explain the chart construction. The structure of a P&F chart revolves around two simple elements: X's and O's.

Figure 8.1: Image of P&F Columns

- **X's:** Represent price movements that are rising (an uptrend).
- **O's:** Represent price movements that are falling (a downtrend).
- **Box Size:** The box size is a predefined amount of price movement required to plot a new X or O. For example, if the box-size is set to 10 points, the price needs to move by 10 points to add another X or O.
- **Reversals** occur when the price moves against the current trend by a certain multiple of the box size (commonly, 3 boxes). For instance, if the price rises by 30 points and then falls by 30 points, the chart will begin a new column of O's.

The beauty of P&F charts lies in their simplicity. Ignoring minor fluctuations allows them to concentrate on significant price movements, making it simpler for traders to observe trends, breakouts, and reversals. By using multi-timeframe analysis with P&F charts, you can align your trades with the larger trend while refining your entries and exits based on price action.

Trading momentum and multi-timeframe

Momentum is the heartbeat of trading. It has what allows trends to persist, and it is the lifeblood of swing and intraday trading. When momentum is strong, we want to enter trades and ride the wave for as long as possible. But as markets move across different timeframes, it becomes essential to use multi-timeframe analysis to see the full picture.

Multi-timeframe trading is the practice of analyzing price action across various timeframes. The main concept is straightforward: recognize the larger trend on a higher timeframe and refine your entry and exit points on a lower timeframe. For example, on a candlestick chart, the weekly chart might show a strong uptrend, while the daily chart shows an entry point after a minor pullback. By aligning your trades with the overall market momentum, you increase the odds of success.

In multi-timeframe analysis, the **higher box-size** (1% or 3% Daily) helps you identify the broad trend, while the **lower box-size** (0.25% Daily) helps you pinpoint the best entry points. Using P&F charts, you can objectively implement the concept of multi-timeframe trading. This helps you trade with more confidence, ensuring that your trades are aligned with the broader trend while taking advantage of precise entry opportunities.

Trading with P&F Charts

The strength of multi-timeframe trading lies in its ability to combine a broad view of the market with precise trade execution. The key is understanding the trend on a higher timeframe and then drilling down to a lower timeframe for optimal entry points. Here's how to apply this concept using P&F charts:

Step 1: Identify the Primary Trend on the Higher Timeframe (3% Daily)

First, start by analyzing the 3% Daily to understand the broader trend. This chart represents the "big picture" and gives you a sense of whether the market is in an uptrend or downtrend.

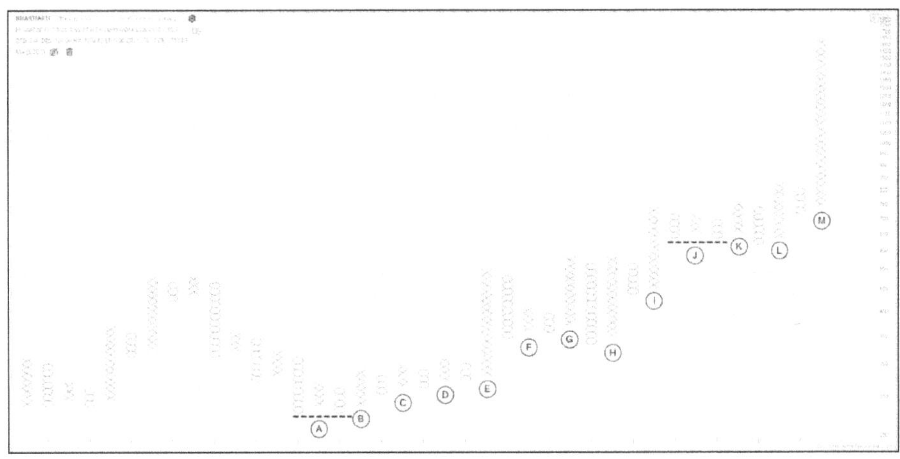

Figure 8.2: Image of P&F Chart

- **Column of X's (Uptrend):** If the chart is in a column of X's, the price is in an uptrend.
- Points B, C, D, E, F, G, H, I, K, L, M mark the columns of 'X' and show an uptrend.
- **O's at Same Level (Support):** If the price forms O's at the same level as previous O's, it suggests the formation of a support, showing that the price might reverse back upward.
- Points A and J are O's at the same level
- **Price Above 20-column Moving Average:** As a final confirmation, make sure the price is above the 20-column moving average. This helps validate the strength of the trend.

By analyzing the 3% Daily, you are focusing on the larger trend and ensuring that your trades are aligned with the overall market direction. This safeguards you from trading against the prevailing trend and helps you maximize your potential profits.

Step 2: Confirm the Trend on the Intermediate Timeframe (1% Daily)

Once you have determined the primary trend on the higher timeframe, switch to the 1% Daily to confirm the trend and breakout signal.

- **Double-Top Buy Pattern**: We look for an active double-top buy breakout. The Double Top Buy pattern means that the market has tested a resistance level twice. If it breaks through, it is expected to keep rising. It is a straightforward and reliable pattern that helps you identify bullish opportunities in the market. This signal confirms the ongoing uptrend. I have explained this pattern in the next section of this chapter.
- **Trend confirmation using MA:** Confirm the trend's strength by ensuring that the breakout is above the 20-column moving average.

This intermediate timeframe is where you confirm that the momentum and the instrument which we are analysing is in the path of least resistance and aligned in the direction of higher timeframe.

Step 3: Fine-tune entries using the lower timeframe (0.25% Daily)

Finally, 0.25% Daily helps pinpoint the perfect entry. This timeframe allows you to spot shallow pullbacks in the direction of higher timeframes (1% and 3% Daily):

- Find shallow pullbacks that are forming fewer boxes in the O column. This indicates that the price has retraced momentarily but is likely to resume its upward momentum.
- Enter the trade when a double-top buy breakout forms after the shallow pullback.
- RSI Above 50: As an additional confirmation of momentum, make sure the RSI is above 50 to ensure that momentum is on your side.

This final step helps you time your entry with precision, allowing you to take advantage of small pullbacks before the price resumes its upward trend. By combining signals from multiple timeframes, you are entering trades with more confidence and precision.

Until now, we have discussed broad concepts of multi-timeframe analysis using P&F charts. It's important for us to delve deeper into the concepts using a more objective approach.

Key Patterns for Multi-timeframe Momentum Trading

P&F charts offer clear and identifiable patterns, making them an excellent choice for momentum traders. These are the essential patterns to consider during multi-timeframe momentum trading.

1. Double-Top Buy (DTB) Pattern

Double-Top Buy is a bullish breakout signal. This pattern forms when the price breaks above a previous high, signalling that the bulls are in control and the price is likely to continue rising. Traders depend on this pattern to validate entering long positions.

How it works: The price forms a column of X, which represents rising prices. After a pullback (shown by a column of O), the price starts rising again. When the new column of X surpasses the previous high, it confirms the Double-Top Buy pattern.

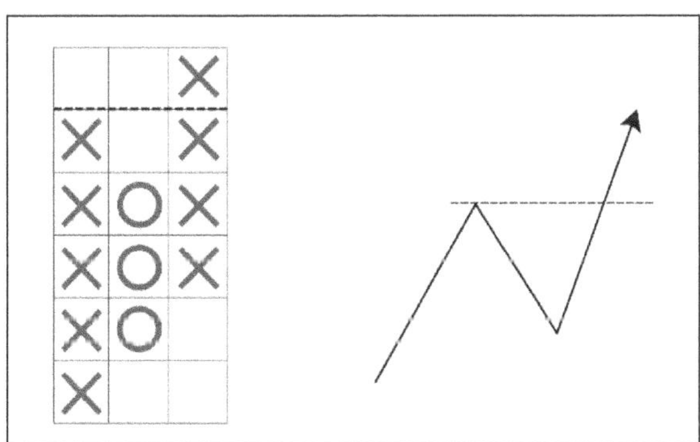

Figure 8.3: Image of Double Top Buy (DTB) pattern

2. Double-Bottom Sell (DBS) Pattern

The Double-Bottom Sell is the bearish counterpart to the Double-Top Buy pattern. This pattern occurs when the price breaks below a previous low, indicating that the bears have gained control and the price is likely to continue falling. Traders frequently use it to initiate short positions or exit long positions.

How it works: The price forms a column of O, which represents falling prices. After a temporary rise (shown by a column of X), the price resumes its decline. When this new column of O drops below the previous low, the Double-Bottom Sell Breakout is confirmed.

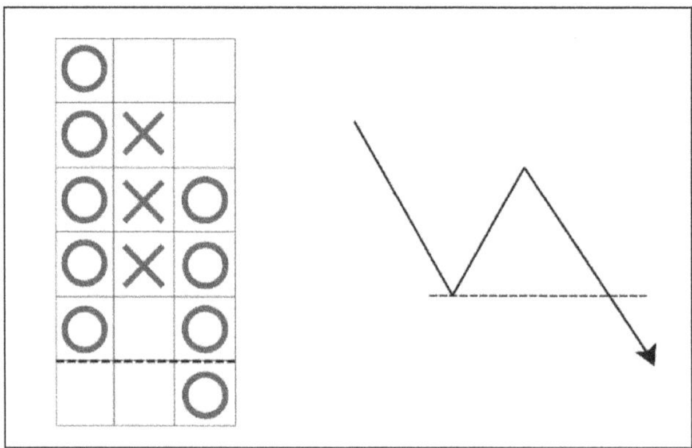

Figure 8.4: Image of Double Bottom Sell (DBS) pattern

3. Shallow Pullbacks

In multi-timeframe trading, shallow pullbacks are crucial for timing entries in an ongoing trend. A shallow pullback indicates a temporary retracement in the dominant trend, providing an ideal entry point to ride the momentum. On P&F charts, these pullbacks consist of 10 boxes or fewer in the opposite direction before the price resumes its original trend.

How it works: Imagine a stock in an uptrend represented by a column of X. The price pulls back slightly, forming a short column of O. When the price starts rising again, forming a new column of X's, it signals that the pullback is over, and the trend is likely to continue.

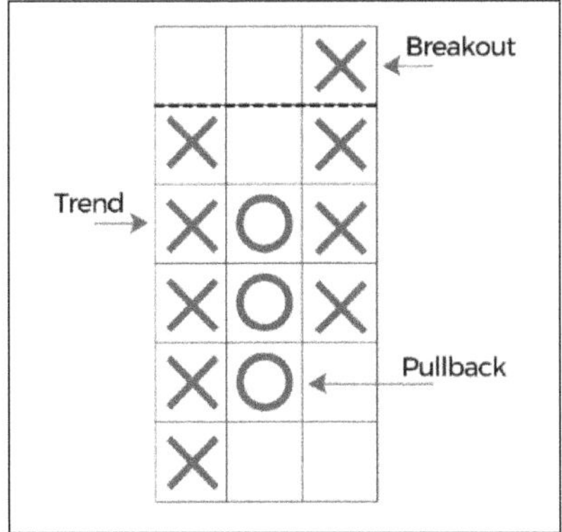

Figure 8.5: Image of shallow pullback

4. Modified High Pole (MHP)

The High Pole pattern occurs when the price moves up significantly (typically 5 boxes or more from DTB) and then retraces over 50% of that upward movement. To avoid being stopped out too soon or prematurely, we use a Modified High Pole. In this variation, the price must move at least 10 boxes in favor of the breakout before a retracement of over 50% triggers an exit. This modification helps ensure that minor price fluctuations do not lead to unnecessary exits.

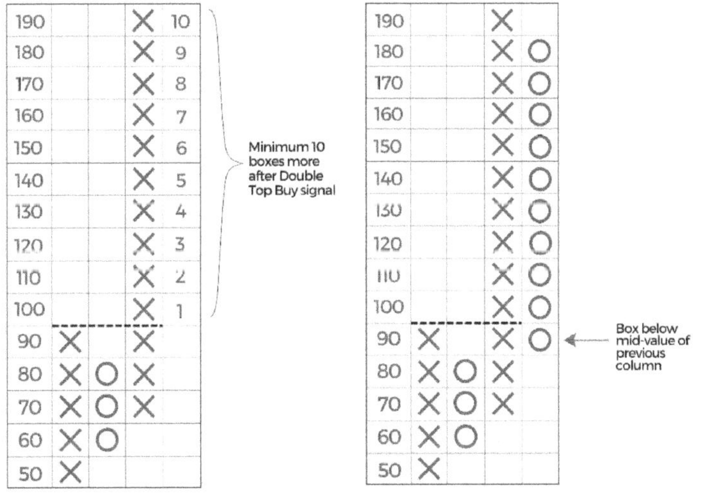

Figure 8.6: Image of Modified High Pole (MHP) pattern

How it works: After a strong upward movement (10 or more boxes), the price retraces by over 50% of that move. If this retracement occurs, it triggers an exit from the position, protecting profits in case of a reversal.

P&F Multi Time-frame Trading Strategy

Let us lay out a strategy that combines multi-timeframe analysis with P&F charts. The core idea here is to participate in the higher timeframe trend, but with precise entries on lower timeframes. This approach helps traders align their trades with the broader trend while using lower timeframes for better entry points and risk management.

Higher Timeframe (3% Daily)

On the higher timeframe, your focus is on identifying the overall trend and ensuring that it is moving in your desired direction. The long-term chart of the market's direction is the 3% Daily, which we use. What we are looking for on 3% Daily timeframe charts are as follows:

- Price to be in a column of X, which signifies an uptrend.
- Examine whether a column of O at the same level has found support at the same price level, implying that support is forming and the price may reverse upward.
- Confirm that the price is above the 20-column moving average to ensure a strong trend.

The rules for the higher timeframe are:

1. Price is forming **O's at the same level**, or
2. The last column is of **X**
3. Price must have **closed above the 20-column moving average**

Either condition 1 or 2 must be met, along with the mandatory requirement of condition 3

These signals give a clear indication of long-term support and momentum, setting the stage for entries in lower timeframes.

Intermediate Timeframe (1% Daily)

On the intermediate timeframe, we confirm the trend and look for specific breakout signals that align with the larger trend on the higher timeframe. Use the 1% Daily P&F chart to identify opportunities for breakout trades:

- We look for an active double-top buy breakout. The Double Top Buy pattern means that the market has tested a resistance level twice. If it breaks through, it is expected to keep rising.
- Confirm that the price is above the 20-column moving average to ensure a strong and unbroken trend on this timeframe.

It is necessary to meet both conditions 1 and 2:

1. Active Double-top buy pattern
2. Price must be above the 20-column moving average.

Aligning the breakout points on the 1% and 3% charts confirms the strong momentum across both timeframes, giving you a better chance of succeeding.

Lower Timeframe (0.25% Daily)

The 0.25% Daily is where you find precise entry points after shallow pullbacks. The goal is to time trades after small reversals to capture momentum. Here's what to look for:

- **Shallow Pullbacks**: Look for pullbacks of 10 boxes or less in the opposite direction (column of O) to confirm that the pullback is shallow and temporary. Pullbacks of over 11 boxes indicate a deeper correction, which may not be ideal for momentum trades.
- **Double-Top Buy Pattern:** After the shallow pullback, wait for a double-top buy breakout to confirm that the price is ready to resume its upward movement.

- Confirm that there has **not been a double-bottom sell** breakout in the shallow retracement column, as this would indicate bearish momentum.
- Confirm that the price is above the 20-column moving average to ensure a strong trend.
- To confirm the momentum, check if the RSI is above 50, showing that the stock is still bullish.

For the 0.25% Daily P&F chart, follow these rules:

1. There is no double-top buy at the current moment.
2. Less than 11 boxes are in the pullback (a maximum of 10 boxes in the column of O's).
3. Double-top buy breakout as your trigger.
4. There should be no double-bottom sell breakout before the buy signal.
5. Price above 20-column moving average.
6. RSI above 50.

These conditions help you enter trades at the best time after a pullback, making sure you are going with the momentum.

Stop-Loss and Trailing Exit Strategy

A critical aspect of any trading system is how you manage risk, and this multi-timeframe P&F trading strategy is no exception. In this strategy, we employ two types of stop-loss and trailing exit mechanisms: Double Bottom Sell Patterns and a Modified High Pole (HP), designed to minimize losses and protect profits as the trade progresses.

Double Bottom Sell as Stop-Loss

When your entry is activated (typically by a Double-Top Buy pattern on the lower timeframe), the subsequent Double Bottom Sell pattern acts as your initial stop-loss. Here's how it works:

- **Initial Stop-Loss:** After you enter the trade, set your stop-loss at the level where the next Double Bottom Sell (DBS) pattern forms. A DBS pattern indicates a bearish reversal on the chart, and if the price hits this level, it suggests the momentum has shifted downward. This would be your exit point to minimize losses.

- **Trailing Stop:** As the trade progresses and more Double Bottom Sell patterns form, these new DBS patterns become your **trailing stop** levels. This allows you to lock in profits as the trade moves in your favour. You adjust the trailing stop upwards with each new column of X (price rising) and subsequent new Double Bottom Sell (column of O).

This approach ensures that you stay in the trade as long as the trend remains intact but exit when a significant bearish signal appears, protecting your gains.

Modified High Pole (MHP) as Trailing Stop

The High Pole (HP) pattern is another critical component of your exit strategy, particularly for locking in profits during a strong upward move. A High Pole occurs when the price moves significantly in one direction (at least 5 boxes after DTB) and then retraces over 50% of that move, signalling potential weakness in the trend. In order to minimize the frequency of getting stopped out from regular High Poles, we implement a more efficient trailing stop called the Modified High Pole (MHP).

In P&F charting, a regular High Pole forms when the price moves up by a minimum of 5 boxes in the direction of the Double-Top Buy pattern and then retraces by over 50% of that upward movement. In volatile markets, you may encounter multiple High Poles that can stop you out prematurely.

To avoid this issue of frequently getting stopped out, we introduce the Modified High Pole. In this variation, we wait for the price to move at least 10 boxes in favour of the Double-Top Buy pattern before considering a High Pole retracement. Only when the price retraces over 50% of the column of X's will we mark it as a Modified High Pole and use it as a trailing stop. This change gives the trade more flexibility, so you are less likely to exit early because of small price changes.

How MHP Works: Once the price has moved 10 boxes in favour of the trend and retraces by over 50% of that move, the Modified High Pole (MHP) is triggered, signalling a reversal or consolidation. Use the MHP level as your trailing stop. If the price continues to retrace beyond the MHP level, it is a sign that the uptrend may lose momentum, and you should exit the trade to lock in your profits.

Using a Modified High Pole allows you to remain in a trade longer, especially in markets where brief retracements are common, while still protecting against larger reversals.

Summary of Exit Rules

To summarize, here are the two main exit rules for the system:

1. **Double Bottom Sell as Initial and Trailing Stop:**

   o   After entry, the first Double Bottom Sell (DBS) becomes your stop-loss.

   o   Each subsequent DBS acts as your trailing stop, ensuring you exit if a significant bearish reversal occurs.

2. **Modified High Pole (MHP) as Trailing Stop:**

   o   After a Double-Top Buy entry, wait for the price to move at least 10 boxes in your favor.

   o   If the price retraces over 50% after that 10-box move, a Modified High Pole (MHP) is formed.

   o   Use the MHP as a trailing stop to lock in gains and protect against reversals.

These exit mechanisms offer a balance of flexibility and protection, helping you maximize profit and minimize risk. By using a combination of Double Bottom Sell patterns and Modified High Poles, you can effectively manage your trades in different market conditions and reduce the chances of being prematurely stopped out.

Summary of Strategy Rules

Timeframe	Condition	Description
Higher Timeframe (3% Daily)	O's at the Same Level or column of X at column 0*	Price forms O's at the same level (support) or moves into a column of X (uptrend).
	Price Above 20-column Moving Average at Column 0	The price must close above the 20-column moving average to confirm the uptrend.
Intermediate Timeframe (1% Daily)	Double-Top Buy Breakout at Column 0	The price has broken above the previous resistance level, indicating a bullish breakout.
	Price Above 20-column Moving Average at Column 0	The breakout must occur above the 20-column moving average to ensure trend strength.
Lower Timeframe (0.25% Daily)	Column of 'O' is not greater than 10 boxes at Column 1 (Shallow Pullbacks)	Look for pullbacks of 10 boxes or lesser (O) indicating a temporary retracement.
	Not a Double-Top Buy at Column 0	Price is in the column of 'X' but has not given the breakout

	RSI Above 50	RSI must be above 50, confirming momentum in the stock.
Entry Trigger	Double-Top Buy Breakout	Enter the trade when a double-top buy breakout forms after the pullback.
Stop-Loss and Trailing Exit	Double Bottom Sell Patterns	The first Double Bottom Sell pattern serves as the initial stop-loss, and subsequent ones act as trailing stops.
	Modified High Pole (MHP)	Wait for a 10-box move in favour of the trade; exit when the price retraces more than 50% of the column of X.

*Column 0 is the most recent column, and Column 1 is the one just before it, and so on.

Case Study: Indian Energy Exchange (IEX)

Let us dive into an example of a multi-timeframe P&F strategy. By methodically aligning different timeframes, we will see how you can spot the right entry points, manage your trade effectively, and ride the trend with confidence.

We begin with the 3% Daily P&F chart, which is like our map for the journey. Here, IEX was in a column of X (marked at point A), signalling a strong uptrend. The bulls' control is evident from this initial clue. Think of the 3% chart as setting the stage—it tells us the overall direction where the stock is likely headed. With the price moving up on this higher timeframe, we are now on the lookout for buying opportunities on the lower timeframes.

Next, we zoom into the 1% Daily chart, where we get our first concrete signal—a Double Top Buy (DTB) pattern at 197 on around 28/08/2024 (marked at point B). This pattern is like a green light, confirming that the uptrend we saw on the 3% chart is solid. Imagine two road signs pointing in the same direction—one in the distance (the 3% chart) and one much closer (the 1% chart). This gives us the confidence to start looking for an even more precise entry on the smallest timeframe.

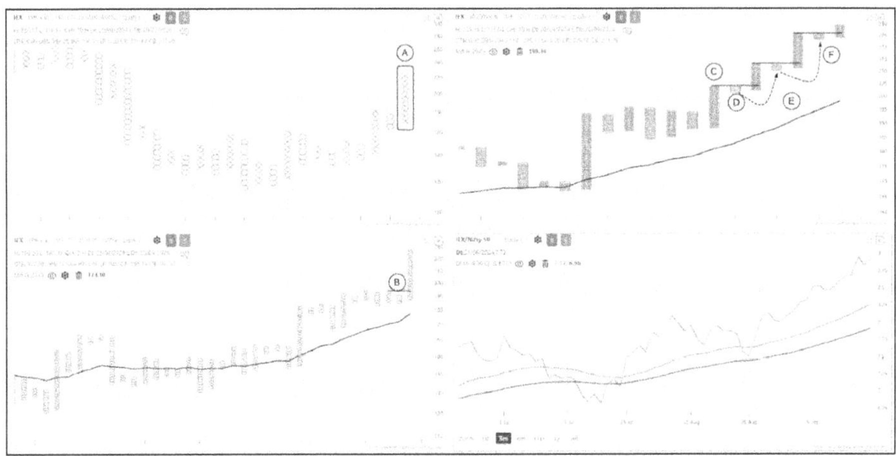

Figure 8.7: Daily timeframe multi-box chart of IEX with 20-column EMA and daily timeframe Ratio chart along with 30-period and 60-period EMA

Now, let us get into the nitty-gritty with the 0.25% Daily P&F chart, where we pull the trigger on the trade. IEX triggered the first DTB pattern here at 206.10 (marked at point C), setting an initial stop loss at 203 (marked at point D). As the trade moved in our favour, we did not sit back—we adjusted our stop loss to lock in profits. When the next DTB pattern appeared at 215, we moved our stop loss up to 211.84 (marked at point E). This trailing stop approach is key because it protects your gains while still giving the trade room to breathe. And the story does not end there. We saw another DTB at 228.31, giving us a new trailing stop at 224.92 (marked at point F).

However, another aspect of this trade is relative strength. Throughout this period, IEX was outperforming the Nifty 50 index. We could see this in the relative strength chart where the 30 EMA remained above the 60 EMA, and the ratio line was also above the 60 EMA. This indicated that IEX not only had an upward trend, but was outperforming the broader market. This extra confirmation added even more conviction to our decision to stay long in the trade.

In this case study, we have seen how the multi-timeframe P&F strategy comes together like a well-rehearsed performance. The higher timeframe sets the tone, the intermediate timeframe confirms the direction, and the lower timeframe gives us the precision to enter and manage the trade. By trailing the stop loss as the trade progresses, we lock in profits while still capturing as much of the trend as possible. And with relative strength on our side, we are confident that we are on the right track.

Trade Summary Table

Timeframe	Entry Price (DTB)	Stop Loss	Summary
0.25% Daily P&F	206.10	203 (Initial)	Initial Entry
	215.00	211.84 (Trailing SL)	Scope to trail SL
	228.31	224.92 (Trailing SL)	Scope to trail SL
1% Daily P&F	197	Not Applicable	Trailed on 0.25% chart
3% Daily P&F	Confirming uptrend	Not Applicable	Managed on lower timeframes

This table breaks down the key actions in the trade, showing how we moved from one entry point to the next, adjusting our stop loss to protect profits along the way. Each row gives you a snapshot of where we entered, where we set our initial stop, and how we trailed it to stay in the game as long as possible.

In summary, this case study is not just about catching a good trade—it is about learning how to do it with a plan, using tools and strategies that give you an edge. With the multi-timeframe P&F strategy, you are not reacting to the market; you are anticipating it, positioning yourself to ride the trend with discipline and confidence.

Case Study: Bombay Stock Exchange

BSE is our subject this time. By carefully aligning various timeframes, we will uncover how this approach helps us spot optimal entry points, manage the trade effectively, and ride the trend confidently.

We start our analysis with the 3% Daily P&F chart, which, as usual, serves as our roadmap. On this chart, BSE entered a column of X at 2594 on August 8, 2024, as marked at point A. This move signalled the beginning of an uptrend on the higher timeframe, with the bulls taking control. Think of the 3% chart as setting the stage, giving us a broad view of the stock's direction. With the price moving up on this larger scale, it is to narrow our focus and look for buying opportunities on the lower timeframes.

On the 1% Daily P&F chart, we see a Double Top Buy pattern at 2672 on August 16, 2024, confirming the solid and continuing uptrend identified on the 3% chart.

Now, let us get into the finer details with the 0.25% Daily P&F chart, where we execute the trade. The first DTB pattern on this chart triggered at 2745, and we set an initial stop loss at 2697 (marked at point C). As the trade moved in our favour, we did not just sit back; we actively managed the position by trailing the stop loss to lock in profits. The next DTB pattern at 2835 allowed us to move our stop loss up to 2731 (point D), ensuring that we captured gains while still letting the trade breathe. As the price continued to rise, we saw another DTB at 2892, which enabled us to trail the stop to 2821 (point E).

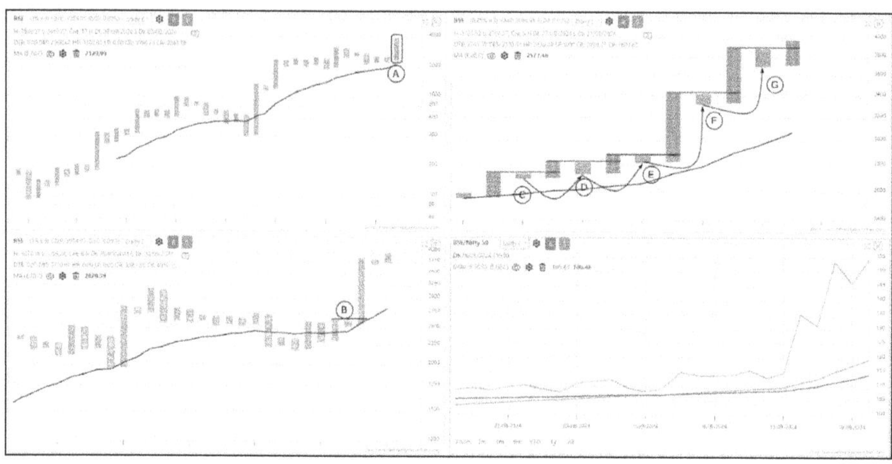

Figure 8.8: Daily timeframe multi-box chart of BSE with 20-column EMA and daily timeframe Ratio chart along with 30-period and 60-period EMA

But the trade did not stop there. BSE continued its upward momentum, and we had the chance to trail our stop loss even further. When the stock hit 3436, we moved the stop loss to 3327 (point F). And the latest development shows a DTB at 3903, allowing us to set a new trailing stop at 3704 (point G). This trade is still ongoing, and we are smoothly riding the trend with each change.

An important aspect of this trade is the relative strength of BSE against the Nifty 50 index. Throughout this period, BSE has outperformed Nifty 50, as evidenced by the 30 EMA staying above the 60 EMA on the relative strength chart. The ratio line also remained above the 60 EMA, signalling that BSE's performance was stronger than the broader market.

Trade Summary Table

Timeframe	Entry Price (DTB)	Stop Loss (Initial)	Summary
0.25% Daily P&F	2745	2697 (Initial)	Initial SL

	2835	2731 (Trailing SL)	Scope to trail SL
	2892	2821 (Trailing SL)	Scope to trail SL
	3436	3327 (Trailing SL)	Scope to trail SL
	3903	3704 (Trailing SL)	Trade still ongoing
1% Daily P&F	2672	Not Applicable	Trailed on 0.25% chart
3% Daily P&F	Confirming uptrend	Not Applicable	Managed on lower timeframes

This table provides a clear summary of our entries, initial stop losses, and how we trailed our stops as the trade progressed. Each row captures a step in the journey, showing how the strategy evolves to lock in profits while allowing the trade to continue riding the trend.

In conclusion, this case study is a testament to how effective a well-structured, multi-timeframe P&F strategy can be. By aligning different timeframes and managing the trade with precision, we can confidently navigate the markets and capture sustained trends, just like we have done with BSE.

Conclusion

The beauty of the multi-timeframe P&F strategy lies in its simplicity and precision. By aligning your trades with the direction of the higher timeframe, you ensure you are always swimming with the current, not against it. With this approach, you can enter the market confidently by making precise entries on shorter timeframes and keeping your stop losses tight. The goal is to participate in the bigger trend while putting only limited risk on the table.

However, strategy is not solely about rules. That is why I encourage you to observe at least 50 trades before executing this strategy in the real markets. This observation and forward testing will give you the conviction you need to trust the process. As you watch the strategy unfold across different trades, you will see how it helps you ride trends smoothly, without the emotional turmoil that often comes with trading.

Remember, trading is as much about managing your mindset as it is about managing your trades. By observing and practicing this strategy, you will be better equipped to stick to your plan, stay disciplined, and make more informed decisions in the heat of the moment. So, take your time, test the strategy, and watch how it can transform your approach to trading.

Chapter 9

TRADING SINGLE CANDLE BREAKOUT USING BOLLINGER BANDS

When I first began trading in my early years, I found it fascinating that there were always a few stocks that could consistently move 5% to 10% in just 4-5 days. I wondered how one could consistently capture these kinds of moves using an objective trading strategy. It felt like a secret that only a select few traders knew, and I was determined to uncover it.

During my initial exploration, I dove into various momentum indicators like RSI, MACD, and Bollinger Bands, among others. However, despite my efforts, I struggled to crack the code. Each strategy seemed to have too many moving parts, making it difficult to create a cohesive, reliable approach. It was like working on a puzzle where the pieces never quite fit together.

As my trading journey progressed, I discovered the concept of Relative Strength, and something clicked. I began to connect the dots, taking the first principles I had learned from the indicators I had studied and practiced for years. Slowly, the missing pieces of the puzzle started to fall into place, forming a clear and actionable strategy that I am excited to share with you in this chapter.

The core principles of any concept, be it in trading or in life, hold immense power. They serve as the foundational building blocks, and once you understand and start implementing them, they work like a well-oiled machine. In this chapter, I aim to convey the essence of these first principles through the lens of my years of experience. I will walk you through the fundamental rules and illustrate them with a strategy that both study and practice have shaped.

Introduction to Bollinger Bands

Bollinger Bands are a powerful and extensively used tool in technical analysis, created by John Bollinger. These bands include three lines: an upper band, a lower band, and a middle band, commonly a simple moving average (SMA) of the price. By using Bollinger Bands, traders can measure market volatility and gain insights into overbought and oversold conditions. Bollinger Bands adapt to market conditions by using standard deviation to create a changing range around the price.

To truly appreciate the utility of Bollinger Bands, it's essential to grasp the concept of standard deviation. Standard deviation is a statistical measure that quantifies the amount of variation or dispersion in a set of data points. In financial markets, it helps assess price fluctuation from its average value over a specific period.

- **Standard Deviation (σ):** It measures how much the prices of an asset deviate from the average price (mean) over a set period. Significant price volatility is indicated by a high standard deviation, while a low standard deviation suggests lower volatility.
- **Application:** Bollinger Bands apply standard deviation to moving averages, resulting in a range that changes based on market volatility. During periods of high volatility, the bands widen, and during periods of low volatility, they narrow.

Logic of Standard Deviations

A key principle of Bollinger Bands is that most data points, approximately 95%, fall within two standard deviations of the mean in a normal distribution. This principle is crucial to understanding how Bollinger Bands function:

- **Upper Band**: Commonly set at two standard deviations above the moving average, representing a level where the asset might be overbought. However, when the price closes above this band, it can indicate a strong momentum in the market.
- **Lower Band**: Set at two standard deviations below the moving average, this band suggests that the asset may be oversold. A price closing below this band often signals a potential reversal or strong downward momentum.
- **Middle Band (SMA):** The middle band, usually a 20-period SMA, serves as a baseline for the calculation of the upper and lower bands. It helps to average out price data and shows the average price over a specific period, giving a point of reference for price's relationship with the Bollinger Bands.

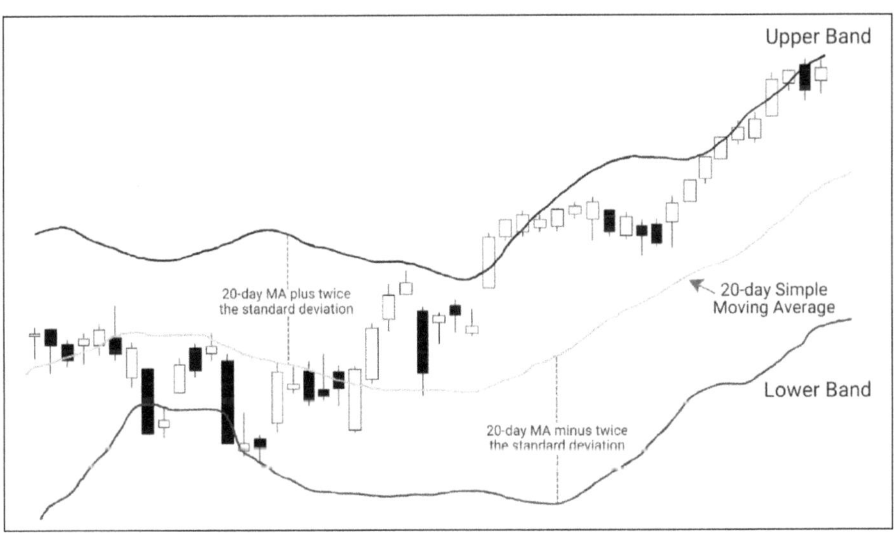

Figure 9.1: Illustration of Bollinger Band

Understanding the Bollinger Bands Squeeze and Breakout

The image illustrates a common phenomenon in trading known as the Bollinger Bands Squeeze. This occurs when the distance between the upper and lower Bollinger Bands narrows, indicating a period of low volatility in the market. During this phase, the price often trades sideways, and the bands appear to contract, as shown in the "Contraction" and "Squeeze" phases in the image.

The price contraction signals that the instrument is preparing for a significant move. Following a period of compression, the price eventually breaks out in one direction, often with higher volatility, as seen in the sharp movement depicted in the "Breakout" phase on the right side of the image.

In our strategy, we aim to participate specifically in this breakout phase, where the price moves rapidly after the squeeze. Here is how it ties into our approach:

1. **Contraction Phase**: During this period of low volatility, the market is quiet, and the price moves within a narrow range. The Bollinger Bands contract, coming closer together, indicating a buildup of energy that will possibly lead to a breakout.

2. **Squeeze Phase**: As the bands tighten, we prepare by closely monitoring the price action. Although we have not made a trade yet, we are staying alert, aware that a significant opportunity may arise soon.

3. **Breakout Phase**: This is where our strategy shines. As the price breaks out of the contraction and squeezes the upper Bollinger Band, we watch for a candle that closes above the band. Once the next candle breaks above the high of this breakout candle, we enter the trade. The idea is to capture this sharp movement, leveraging the momentum that follows the breakout. I will share the trade participation rules in the next part of the chapter.

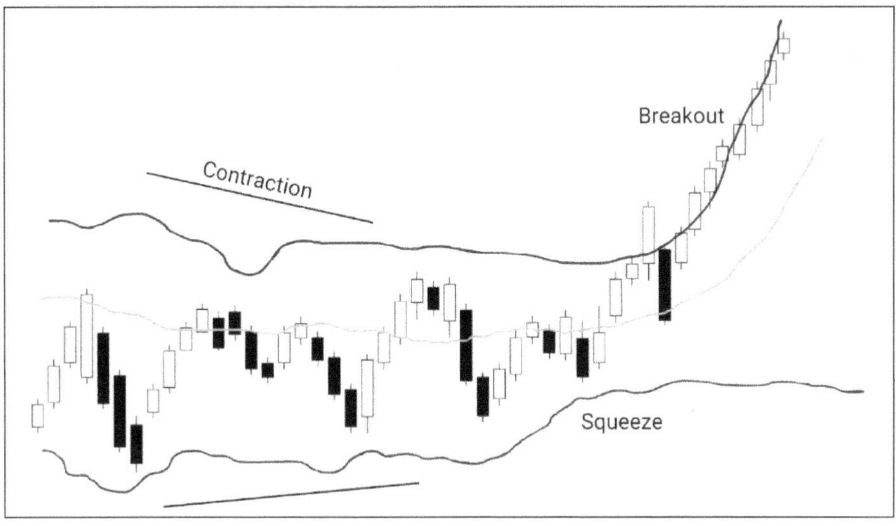

Figure 9.2: Illustration of Bollinger Band squeeze

Trading Single Candle Breakout using Bollinger Bands

After a strong foundation in the principles of Bollinger Bands, Band Squeeze, and standard deviation, we can now delve into a distinctive trading strategy known as the Single Candle Breakout. I have perfected and traded this strategy over the years, and it capitalizes on momentum when the price breaks above the high of the preceding candle. Yet, implementing this strategy requires more finesse than trading every time this condition is satisfied.

The strategy revolves around entering a trade when the price exceeds the high of the preceding candle. The key to success is verifying the breakout with Bollinger Bands, Relative Strength Index (RSI), and Relative Strength to enhance the trade's potential and avoid false signals.

How the Single Candle Breakout Strategy Works

Identify the Setup

The first step is to monitor price action closely to identify a potential breakout scenario. Look for a candle that suggests a continuation in the direction of the breakout, indicating that momentum will carry the price further.

Confirmation with Bollinger Bands

Before making a trade, it is crucial to confirm the breakout by checking its relationship with the Bollinger Bands. As discussed earlier, price action typically remains within the bands formed by two standard deviations from the moving average. If the price closes above the upper Bollinger Band, it usually indicates strong momentum rather than an overbought condition.

However, to refine the entry timing for this strategy, we use Bollinger Bands set at 1.5 standard deviations instead of the usual 2. This change ensures that we are not too late with the entry, allowing us to capture a quick swing move in the direction of the trend. By doing so, we can enter the trade at an earlier stage of the breakout, increasing the likelihood of participating in the strongest part of the price movement. Key insight is a close above the upper Bollinger Band, thus signalling significant buying pressure and suggesting that the breakout is likely to lead to a continued upward movement.

Confirmation with Relative Strength Index (RSI)

To further validate the breakout, examine the Relative Strength Index (RSI) on the same timeframe you are trading. For this strategy, it is crucial to focus on stocks that have an RSI above 60. When the RSI is above 60, it means the stock has strong momentum for a breakout, which improves the chances of a successful trade. By using this momentum-based confirmation, you can eliminate weaker setups and increase the chances of entering trades that will continue.

Confirmation with Relative Strength

The final layer of confirmation comes from analyzing the stock's relative strength compared to the broader market, the Nifty 50 index. Trade stocks that are relatively outperforming the Nifty 50 Index at the time of the breakout. By using relative strength analysis, you can ensure that you are trading stocks that are not only performing well on their own but also surpassing the broader market. This increases the chances of the breakout leading to a profitable move, as it aligns your trade with the prevailing market strength.

Entry Trigger

After confirming that the price has closed above the upper Bollinger Band (set at 1.5 standard deviations) and ensuring the stock is above 60 RSI and relatively outperforming the Nifty 50 Index, look for the next candle to break above the high of this "breakout candle." This breakout above the preceding candle's high serves as the entry signal. If Candle A closes above the upper Bollinger Band, and meets the RSI and relative strength criteria, you would then wait for Candle B to break above the high of Candle A. Once this happens, it's time to enter the trade.

Stop-Loss Placement

To effectively manage risk, place a stop-loss order just below the low of the breakout candle (referred to as Candle A). This ensures that if the trade does not go as planned and the price reverses, your losses are minimized. The precise placement of the stop-loss is crucial for protecting your capital while giving the trade enough room to develop.

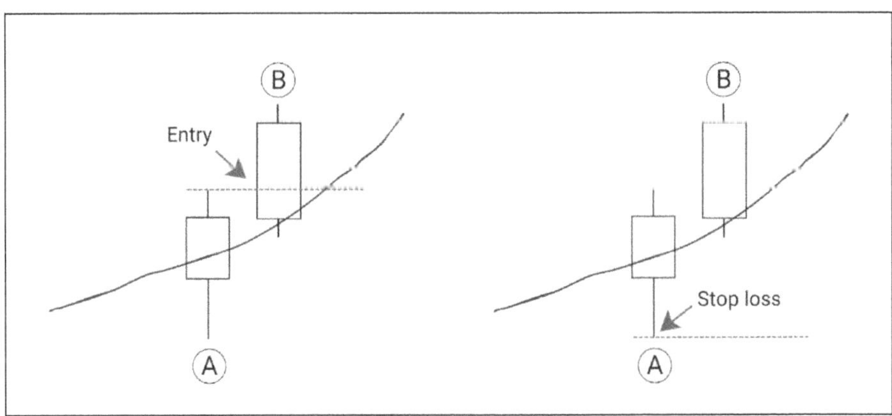

Figure 9.3: Illustration of entry and stop-loss placement

Exit Strategy

The exit strategy for the Single Candle Breakout approach relies on a trailing stop method. Once you enter the trade, make sure to continuously adjust the stop-loss to the lowest low of the preceding two candles. To simplify this process, consider using a 2-period Donchian Channel, which tracks the lowest low of the last two periods on its own. This trailing stop mechanism allows you to capture the ongoing momentum while safeguarding your gains. By keeping the trade open until the stop-loss triggers, you ensure that your profits are maximized as long as the trend continues.

Timeframe Selection

Depending on your trading style, you can apply the Single Candle Breakout strategy across various timeframes. If you are a positional trader who usually holds trades for over four weeks, the weekly timeframe is most suitable. If you are a swing trader, the ideal timeframe for you is the daily, as trades are typically held for a few days to a couple of weeks. Intraday traders, who prefer to open and close trades within the same day, will find the 15-minute timeframe most effective. Regardless of the chosen timeframe, the overall rules of the strategy remain consistent, allowing you to adapt this method to your specific trading style while maintaining its effectiveness.

Trade Targets

I have developed this strategy to capture different target ranges based on your trading style:

- Swing Trading: Aim to capture a move of 5% to 8%.
- Intraday Trading: Target a move of 1% to 3%.
- Positional Trading: Look for a 10% to 20% move.

These target ranges allow you to set realistic expectations based on the timeframe and type of trade you are executing.

Summary of Single Candle Breakout Rules

Rule	Details
Setup Identification	Monitor the price action to identify potential breakout scenarios. Find a candle likely to be breached by the next one.
Bollinger Bands Confirmation	Use Bollinger Bands set at 1.5 standard deviations. Confirm the breakout when the price closes above the upper Bollinger Band, indicating strong momentum.
RSI Confirmation	Ensure the stock's RSI is above 60, suggesting sufficient momentum to support the breakout.
Relative Strength Confirmation	Trade stocks that are outperforming the Nifty 50 Index. Use Relative Strength analysis to ensure the stock is stronger than the broader market.
Entry Trigger	Enter the trade when the next candle breaks above the high of the previous candle (breakout candle).
Stop-Loss Placement	Place the stop-loss just below the low of the breakout candle.
Exit Strategy	Use a trailing stop method by adjusting the stop-loss to the lowest low of the preceding two candles. Use a 2-period Donchian Channel to automate this.
Trade Targets (Expected)	Positional Trading: 10% to 20% - Swing Trading: 5% to 8% - Intraday Trading: 1% to 3%
Timeframe Selection	- Positional Trading: Weekly - Swing Trading: Daily - Intraday Trading: 15-minute

Risk Management	The strategy is designed with an affordable risk-to-reward ratio, but be aware of possible whipsaws.

Case Study: Indian Energy Exchange (IEX)

In this case study, we analyze the Indian Energy Exchange (IEX) within the context of a swing trade, using Relative Strength analysis as a crucial component. The first step in this approach involves identifying stocks that are outperforming the broader market. By plotting the ratio chart of IEX against the Nifty 50 index and overlaying the 30-day and 60-day Exponential Moving Averages (EMAs) on a daily timeframe, we can determine whether the stock is showing relative strength. From May 15, 2024, IEX exhibited signs of relative outperformance, with the 30 EMA crossing above the 60 EMA. This relative strength made IEX a prime candidate for our breakout strategy.

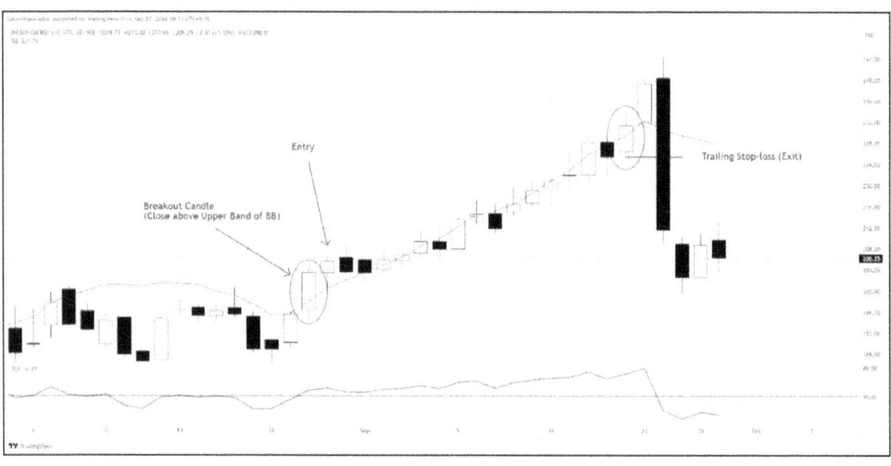

Figure 9.4: Daily timeframe chart of IEX along with Upper Bollinger Band and Relative Strength Index

On August 28, 2024, IEX provided further confirmation when it closed above the upper Bollinger Band, which was set at 1.5 standard deviations to capture quicker moves. This closing price above the upper band indicated strong momentum, supported by an RSI reading of 64, suggesting that the stock had sufficient strength to continue its upward movement.

The next day, on August 29, 2024, the breakout was confirmed as the price moved above the high of the previous day's candle, triggering an entry at 205.45. To manage risk, we placed an initial stop-loss just below the low of the breakout candle at 194.75, ensuring that any adverse movement would result in minimal loss. The calculated risk for this trade was around 5.2%, which is within an acceptable range for this strategy.

As the trade went on, the strategy used a trailing stop-loss method to protect gains and keep making profits. The stop-loss was adjusted to the lowest low of the preceding two candles, which is monitored using a 2-period Donchian Channel. On September 24, 2024, the trailing stop-loss was triggered at 226 when the low of the last two days was breached, signalling the exit from the trade. This exit secured a profit of 20.55 points, translating to a gain of approximately 10% from the entry point.

The structured approach of the Single Candle Breakout Strategy, combined with the use of Relative Strength and RSI for confirmation, enabled you to effectively capture the momentum-driven move in IEX while managing risk through a disciplined stop-loss strategy.

Trade Summary	Details
Timeframe	Daily
Trade Type	Swing Trade
Relative Outperformance Identified	May 15, 2024
RSI Confirmation	August 28, 2024 (RSI at 64)
Bollinger Band Confirmation	August 28, 2024
Entry Trigger	August 29, 2024, at 205.45

Initial Stop-loss	194.75
Risk (in%)	5.2%
Exit Trigger	September 24, 2024, at 226
Total Gains	20.55 points (approximately 10% profit)

Case Study: Bajaj Auto Ltd (BAJAJ-AUTO)

The first step, as always, involves identifying stocks that are relatively outperforming the broader market. By using a ratio chart of Bajaj Auto against the Nifty 50 and overlaying the 30-day and 60-day Exponential Moving Averages (EMAs), we observed that Bajaj Auto began to show signs of relative strength on August 26. This relative outperformance signalled that Bajaj Auto was a strong candidate for our breakout strategy.

On August 23, with the price closing above the upper Bollinger Band, which was set at 1.5 standard deviations. This breakout, coupled with the RSI reading of 72, showed strong momentum behind the move. The following trading session on August 26 provided the entry trigger when the price breached the high of the breakout candle, reaching 10,444.35. To manage risk effectively, we strategically placed an initial stop-loss just below the low of the breakout candle.

As the trade progressed, we employed the trailing stop-loss mechanism, adjusting it to the lowest low of the preceding two candles, to protect gains. On September 5, the breach of the low of the last two days triggered the exit at 10,908. This first trade captured a solid gain, taking advantage of the continued momentum that was initially identified.

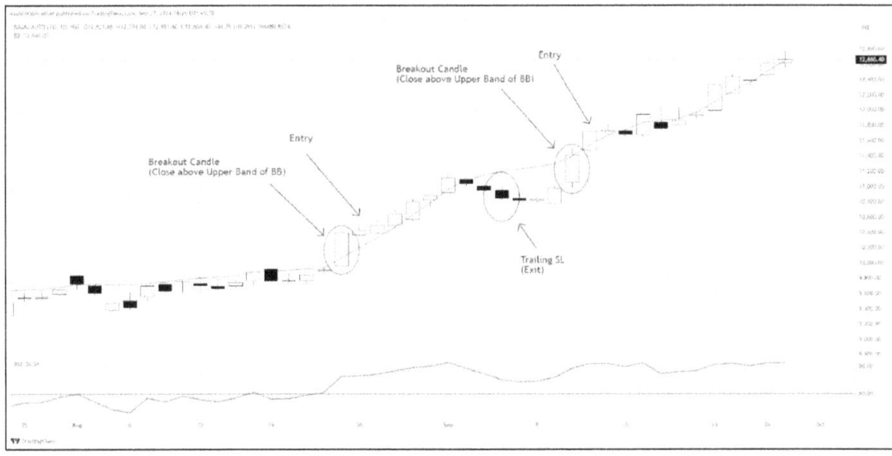

Figure 9.5: Daily timeframe chart of BAJAJAUTO along with Upper Bollinger Band and Relative Strength Index

Interestingly, a fresh breakout in Bajaj Auto occurred soon after. On September 11, we observed another breakout candle, with the RSI even higher at 78.85, suggesting even stronger momentum. The following day, September 12, provided the entry signal when the price breached the high of this breakout candle, entering the trade at 11,501.30. As of now, this trade has not triggered an exit, with the current market price (CMP) at 12,666.

This case study illustrates how the Single Candle Breakout Strategy, combined with Relative Strength, can be effectively applied to capture significant price movements while managing risk. By following a structured approach, the strategy enabled you to enter and exit trades with precision, capitalizing on market momentum.

Trade Summary	Details
Timeframe	Daily
Trade Type	Swing Trade
Relative Outperformance Identified	August 26, 2024
RSI Confirmation (1st Trade)	August 23, 2024 (RSI at 72)

Bollinger Band Confirmation (1st Trade)	August 23, 2024
Entry Trigger (1st Trade)	August 26, 2024, at 10,444.35
Initial Stop-loss (1st Trade)	9,880
Risk (in%) [1st Trade]	5.40%
Exit Trigger (1st Trade)	September 5, 2024, at 10,908
Total Gains (1st Trade)	463.65 points (approx. 4.4% profit)
RSI Confirmation (2nd Trade)	September 11, 2024 (RSI at 78.85)
Bollinger Band Confirmation (2nd Trade)	September 11, 2024
Entry Trigger (2nd Trade)	September 12, 2024, at 11,501.30
Initial Stop-loss (2nd Trade)	10,850
Risk (in%) [2nd Trade]	5.70%
Current Market Price (CMP)	12,666
Total Gains (2nd Trade)	1,164.70 points (approx. 10.1% profit)
Exit Trigger (2nd Trade)	Trade is ongoing

Case Study: Dixon Technologies (India) Ltd (DIXON)

In this case study, we examine positional trade on Dixon Technologies (India) Ltd. Despite the longer timeframe, we maintain consistency by checking the ratio chart on the daily timeframe to ensure relative outperformance against the broader market.

Dixon Technologies showed signs of relative outperformance against the Nifty 50 starting on February 26, 2024. This was identified by analyzing the ratio chart, where the 30 EMA was seen trading above the 60 EMA, indicating the stock's strength relative to the market.

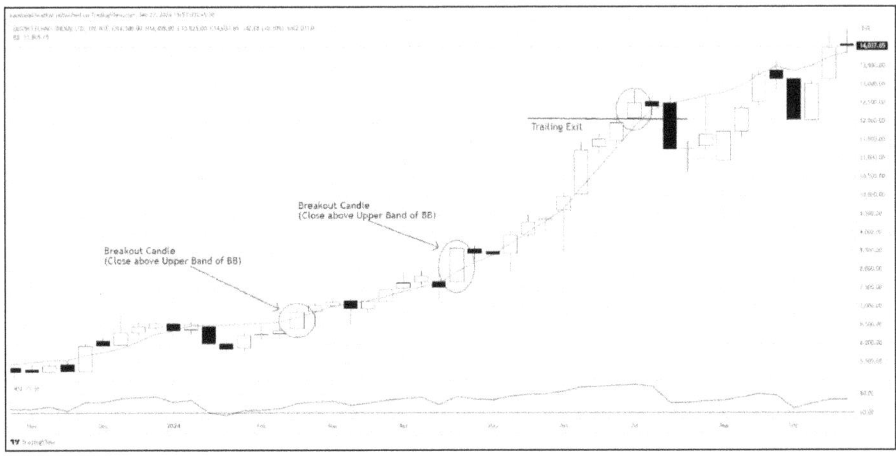

Figure 9.6: Daily timeframe chart of DIXON along with Upper Bollinger Band and Relative Strength Index

The first breakout signal occurred on February 19, 2024, with the RSI at 70.05, signalling strong momentum. On February 26, 2024, the price broke above the high of the breakout candle, triggering the entry for this trade at 6929. To manage risk effectively, an initial stop-loss was set at 6410, just below the low of the breakout candle.

Dixon Technologies maintained strong performance as the trade advanced, utilizing the trailing stop-loss mechanism to secure profits while keeping the trade open. On April 15, 2024, the exit signal was activated due to the price hitting 7480, after breaching the trailing stop condition. This trade generated a 551-point gain, equating to around an 8% profit.

Following this successful trade, Dixon Technologies presented another opportunity for a breakout. The next breakout occurred on April 22, 2024, with a strong bullish candle. The entry was triggered on April 28, 2024, when the price breached the high of the breakout candle at 8607. The initial stop-loss for this trade was set at 7627.45 to protect against any adverse price movements.

As the trade unfolded, Dixon Technologies exhibited significant upward momentum, and the trade remained active for several weeks. Finally, the exit triggered on July 15, 2024, at 12086.45, after a substantial rally.

This trade captured a remarkable gain of 3479.45 points, resulting in a profit of approximately 40%.

This case study shows how well the Single Candle Breakout Strategy works for long-term trades on a weekly basis. By consistently monitoring relative strength on the daily timeframe and following a disciplined approach to entry, stop-loss placement, and exit strategies, traders can successfully capture substantial market moves while managing risk effectively.

Trade Summary	Details
Timeframe	Weekly
Trade Type	Positional Trade
Relative Outperformance Identified	February 26, 2024
RSI Confirmation (1st Trade)	February 19, 2024 (RSI at 70.05)
Bollinger Band Confirmation (1st Trade)	February 19, 2024
Entry Trigger (1st Trade)	February 26, 2024, at 6929
Initial Stop-loss (1st Trade)	6410
Risk (in%) [1st Trade]	7.5%
Exit Trigger (1st Trade)	April 15, 2024, at 7480
Total Gains (1st Trade)	551 points (approx. 8% profit)
RSI Confirmation (2nd Trade)	April 22, 2024
Bollinger Band Confirmation (2nd Trade)	April 22, 2024
Entry Trigger (2nd Trade)	April 28, 2024, at 8607
Initial Stop-loss (2nd Trade)	7627.45
Risk (in%) [2nd Trade]	11.4%
Exit Trigger (2nd Trade)	July 15, 2024, at 12086.45
Total Gains (2nd Trade)	3479.45 points (approx. 40% profit)

Final Thoughts on the Single Candle Breakout Strategy

The Single Candle Breakout Strategy with Bollinger Bands is a robust approach for capturing market momentum. By understanding the core principles of Bollinger Bands and incorporating them with other indicators like the Relative Strength Index (RSI) and Relative Strength against a benchmark index, you can effectively identify and capitalize on breakout opportunities.

You can customize this strategy to fit your trading style, whether it is for short-term, medium-term, or long-term trading. The key to success lies in the disciplined application of the strategy's rules—ensuring that every trade is confirmed by strong momentum and relative outperformance, and that risk is carefully managed through strategic stop-loss placements.

In this chapter, I accentuated the importance of using trailing stop-losses. They safeguard gains and enable trades to maximize profits. This method helps you stay in the trend for longer, so that you can make the most money while avoiding unnecessary risks.

It is important to understand that, while this strategy is strong, it does have its share of challenges. The potential for whipsaws exists, and there will be times when the market does not behave as expected. However, by sticking to the principles outlined in this chapter—confirmation through Bollinger Bands, RSI, and Relative Strength, and disciplined risk management—you can navigate these challenges with confidence.

Before you implement this strategy in live markets, it is advisable to forward-test it by observing 50 trades. This practice will help you build conviction in the system and enable you to handle the emotional ups and downs of trading with greater ease. Remember, the strength of any strategy lies not just in its rules, but in your ability to follow those rules consistently and with discipline.

In trading, as in life, success comes from understanding the fundamentals, applying them consistently, and adapting to new challenges. The Single Candle Breakout Strategy with Bollinger Bands is a tool that, when used correctly, can help you achieve consistent results in the markets.

Chapter 10

TRADING MULTI-YEAR BREAKOUTS

No trading book is complete without addressing the potential of multi-year breakouts. In the realm of technical analysis, few setups offer as strong a signal or as high a probability of success as multi-year and multi-top breakouts. These patterns, which build over extended periods, reveal profound price consolidation and have a reputation for delivering substantial moves once the breakout occurs. This chapter delves into trading multi-year and multi-top breakouts using Point & Figure (P&F) charts, with a specific focus on a 1% box size on the daily timeframe. This box size makes it easier for traders to see important breakout points on the chart, without getting distracted by short-term market noise.

Unlike time-based charts that capture every fluctuation and add noise to price movements, P&F charts allow traders to focus exclusively on price action. This clarity is essential for tracking multi-year and multi-top consolidations, which can signal powerful breakouts after years of build-up. Using a 1% box size on the daily timeframe helps streamline the focus to capture only significant price movements, allowing traders to see significant support and resistance levels and align their trades accordingly.

Understanding Multi-Year and Multi-Top Breakouts

In P&F Charts, multi-year or multi-top breakouts occur after the price has repeatedly approached a key resistance level but could not break through. The continuous inability of the price to break resistance level leads to an extended consolidation period, forming numerous peaks.

A breakout that finally pushes above these levels signals a shift in market sentiment, often leading to a strong upward trend.

Multi-Year Breakouts

A multi-year breakout occurs when the price stays below an important resistance level for several years, repeatedly testing it but not breaking through until a clear breakout happens. This setup is particularly potent, as it reflects a prolonged period of accumulation, followed by a rapid shift to momentum buying once the breakout occurs.

Multi-Top Breakouts

Multi-top breakouts function similarly but form over shorter periods, usually within several months. These patterns are still significant, as they indicate repeated tests of a resistance level. Every time resistance is tested, the range gets tighter. This suggests that momentum is increasing, and when it finally breaks, there will be a big upward movement.

Key Pattern: The Bear-Trap

Bear-traps are one of the most reliable P&F signals, ideal for confirming breakouts from multi-year and multi-top patterns. This four-column bullish pattern occurs when a double-bottom sell pattern reverses into a double-top buy pattern. The initial sell signal is a false breakdown, swiftly followed by a buying signal that traps bearish traders who are forced to cover their positions, further fueling the bullish momentum. The bear-trap serves as a confirmation signal, indicating a potential upward breakout with strong bullish sentiment.

By following these steps and understanding the unique characteristics of multi-year and multi-top breakouts, traders can take advantage of high-probability setups on P&F charts. These setups, particularly when paired with confirmation signals like the bear-trap, offer excellent opportunities to participate in powerful, long-term trends while managing risk effectively.

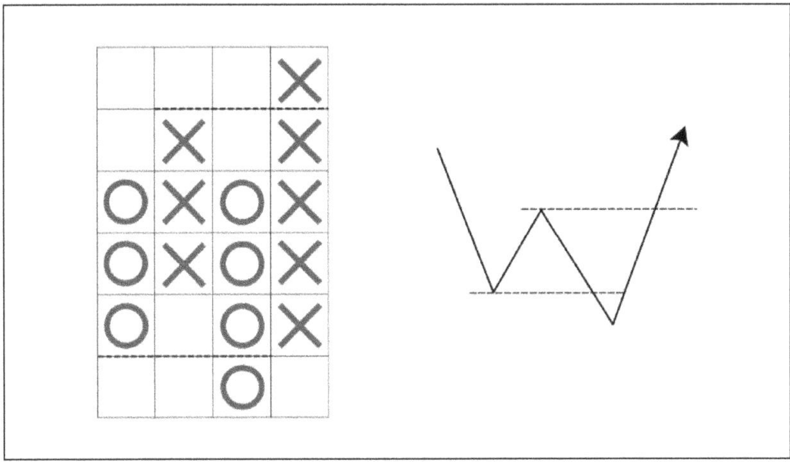

Figure 10.1: Illustration of Bear-trap pattern

Steps to Trading Multi-Year and Multi-Top Breakouts

Step 1: Identify Key Resistance and Pattern Formation

To begin, examine a daily P&F chart with a 1% box size. Identify primary resistance levels where price has encountered significant resistance, yet has failed to break through. For a multi-year breakout, the price should remain below this resistance for three years or longer. For multi-top breakouts, identify areas where price has tested resistance multiple times over a span of several months.

Step 2: Confirm Consolidation or Buildup Near Resistance

Observe whether a tight "buildup" is forming just below or around the resistance level, indicating that the asset is gathering strength for a potential breakout. On a P&F chart, this will appear as columns that gradually converge, forming a base—a signal that the asset may soon break through its resistance with momentum.

Step 3: Execute on the Breakout with Bear-Trap Pattern

When the price forms a breakout column of Xs above the resistance on the P&F chart, it is time to prepare for entry. But instead of entering immediately, it is better to wait for a bear-trap pattern above the breakout level. A bear-trap is formed when there is a breakdown that quickly reverses, indicating that bearish momentum is depleted. The bear-trap provides additional confirmation that the breakout is supported by significant buying interest. It traps bearish traders and shifts momentum to bullish direction.

Step 4: Placing Stop-Loss Orders

Place your stop-loss orders below the bear-trap formation, specifically under the lowest point in the column of 'O'. This allows for typical market fluctuations and helps manage risk by protecting the position if the breakout fails.

Step 5: Setting Targets and Trade Management

To set profit targets, measure the height of the consolidation or buildup zone. Add this measurement to the breakout point to project the target. Traders who want to maximize gains can use trailing stops based on recent lows within the bear-trap formation. This allows for continued upside potential while securing profits. I prefer using trailing stop-loss as it helps to ride the ongoing trend.

Stocks poised for a multi-year breakout

When identifying stocks poised for a multi-year breakout, it can be valuable to look beyond the technical setup and consider specific fundamental metrics that indicate strong business health and growth potential. While these metrics are not strict rules, they serve as powerful filters to help identify fundamentally robust companies likely to sustain upward trends post-breakout.

The following metrics serve as general guidelines for refining stock selection:

1. **PAT Margin (Net Profit Margin) is greater than 5%**
   Companies with a PAT margin above 5% are typically profitable and maintain good control over their costs. This

metric indicates that the company's profitability is sufficient to withstand market fluctuations, making it more likely to sustain upward momentum after a breakout.

2. **3-Year Sales CAGR is greater than 20%**

   A high sales CAGR over three years shows consistent revenue growth, reflecting strong demand and the company's ability to scale. Companies with strong sales growth are better positioned to continue generating interest in the market, supporting the likelihood of a sustained breakout.

3. **EBITDA Margin (Operating Profit Margin) is greater than 10%**

   EBITDA margins above 10% demonstrate operational efficiency, indicating that the company's core business generates sufficient profit. A healthy operating margin provides a buffer against operational risks and shows the company's capacity to reinvest in growth, making it a promising candidate for holding in a breakout trade.

You can use these metrics to choose companies with strong financial and operational performance for multi-year breakouts. While it is possible to execute breakouts without following these metrics strictly, having them adds confidence to the trade. This ensures that the stock's underlying business fundamentals align with its technical setup. This alignment creates a better trading opportunity for traders to benefit from both short-term breakout momentum and long-term business growth potential.

Case Study: Siemens Ltd.

The case study of Siemens Ltd. provides a classic example of a multi-year breakout pattern, perfectly suited for long-term P&F chart analysis. Using a 1% box size on the daily timeframe, this setup demonstrates the power of enduring resistance levels and the potential of a strong, momentum-driven trend once those levels are breached. Siemens Ltd. had been consolidating below the significant resistance levels established in 2015 and 2019. These resistance levels created a horizontal barrier on the P&F chart, signalling multiple tops in the price movement, with the stock unable to cross these levels for nearly six years.

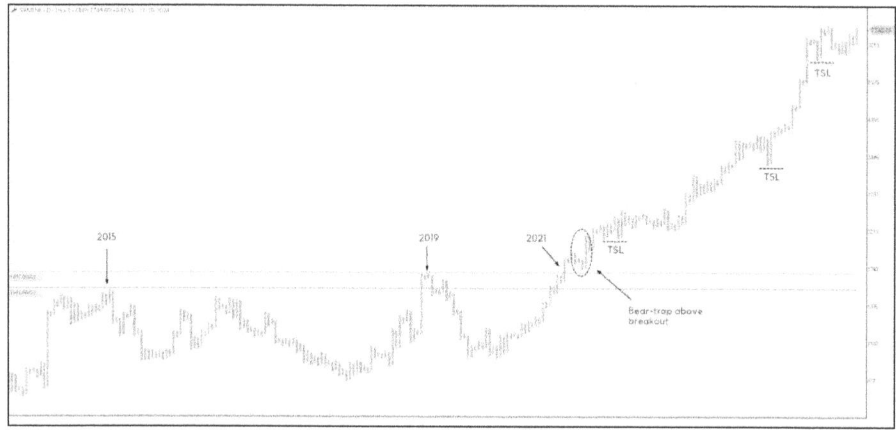

Figure 10.2: Daily timeframe chart of SIEMENS on 1% Box Size

In 2021, Siemens' stock once again approached the resistance zone, testing the patience of traders observing the multi-top formation. Instead of immediately breaking out, the stock consolidated near this level, forming a "buildup" pattern indicative of strength gathering for an eventual breakout. Finally, in 2021, Siemens broke through the long-standing resistance level, with a new column of 'X' on the P&F chart clearly indicating the breakout. This breakout was particularly notable as it was accompanied by a bear-trap pattern—an indication that sellers had tried to push the price lower but failed, only for the price to quickly reverse upward, trapping the bears and adding further conviction to the breakout.

The bear-trap pattern confirmed the breakout and made it more likely that the upward trend would continue. The pattern quickly reversed from a false breakdown, giving traders confidence in the trade's direction. Following the breakout, Siemens' price displayed strong bullish momentum, validating the multi-year breakout thesis.

Once the breakout was in place, traders who entered could apply a trailing stop-loss (TSL) strategy to lock in profits as the trend developed.

The TSL, placed under significant pullback points, allowed traders to ride the upward trend while managing risk effectively. As marked on the chart, there were multiple trailing stop-loss levels where traders could adjust their stops higher as Siemens continued its bullish ascent, providing ample opportunity to maximize gains while minimizing risk.

Throughout this trend, the stock demonstrated the value of patience and strategic trade management. By waiting for the breakout after years of consolidation, and then following the trend with a TSL, traders could capture substantial gains. In this case, Siemens' breakout led to a persistent rally that rewarded those who adhered to the rules of multi-year breakout trading on P&F charts.

Case Study: Apar Industries Ltd.

Here in Apar Industries Ltd., we identified a multi-year breakout with a strong momentum-driven rally by using a P&F chart with a 1% box size on the daily timeframe. This chart setup allowed us to clearly see significant resistance levels established back in 2017 and 2018, when Apar Industries repeatedly tested the 912 level. Each time, however, the stock was unable to break through, signalling a long-term consolidation phase as price failed to move above this multi-year resistance.

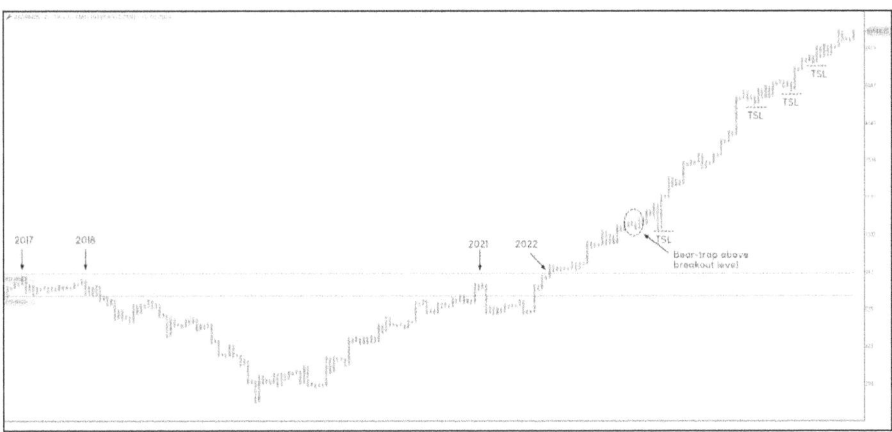

Figure 10.3: Daily timeframe chart of APARIND on 1% Box Size

Years later, in 2021 and 2022, Apar Industries revisited these historical highs, marking a renewed attempt to breach the critical resistance level at 912. The breakout occurred after several tests, with a bear-trap pattern pushing it above the breakout zone. This bear-trap was a key signal indicating the failure of sellers to maintain control, adding to the conviction behind the breakout. Traders relying on P&F charting would recognize this as a high-probability setup, with the bear-trap acting as confirmation of bullish momentum, creating an ideal entry opportunity at the beginning of a potential long-term trend.

Once the breakout was confirmed, traders could strategically apply a trailing stop-loss (TSL) method to manage the trade effectively, as indicated on the chart. Placing TSLs below significant retracement levels allowed traders to ride the trend while minimizing risk. As Apar Industries gained momentum, each new high presented an opportunity to adjust the TSL, locking in profits progressively while letting the trade run.

Case Study: DLF Ltd.

DLF Ltd. offers another exemplary case of a multi-year breakout, as identified on a P&F chart with a 1% box size on the daily timeframe. This pattern unfolded over an extended period, with the stock facing significant resistance around the 242 and 273 levels. DLF first reached these levels in 2014, then revisited them in 2017, and once again in 2020 and 2021, creating a series of resistance points over nearly a decade. These repeated tests without a breakout indicated a prolonged consolidation phase, with the stock unable to sustain a move above these levels.

In 2021, after years of consolidation and multiple resistance attempts, DLF finally broke out above this key resistance area, signalling a significant shift in momentum. This breakout was further validated by the formation of a bear-trap pattern above the resistance level. This bear-trap setup highlighted the failure of sellers to maintain control, thus increasing the likelihood of a sustained upward movement. The bear-trap acted as an ideal entry point, as it confirmed the strength of the breakout and the reversal of sentiment in favour of the bulls.

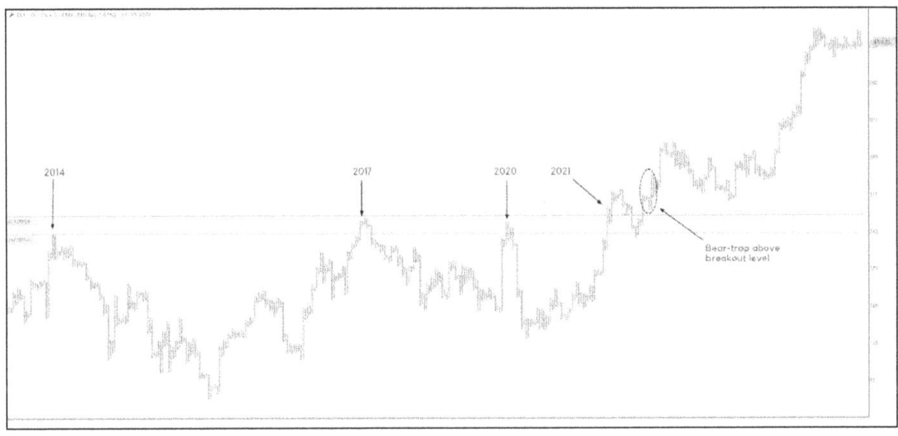

Figure 10.4: Daily timeframe chart of DLF on 1% Box Size

Final Thoughts

In conclusion, multi-year and multi-top breakouts offer some of the most powerful and reliable trading opportunities for those who can patiently await a clear, decisive move beyond long-standing resistance levels. These setups harness the energy accumulated during prolonged consolidation phases, where supply and demand are in equilibrium, and then release it in a swift and often substantial price movement once a breakout occurs. Point & Figure charts, with their unique focus on price action over time, are particularly well-suited to identify these breakouts, filtering out short-term market noise and providing a clear view of significant support and resistance levels.

By using a structured approach—identifying resistance, confirming consolidation near breakout levels, waiting for a confirmed breakout, and setting disciplined trailing stops—traders can capture significant trends with higher probability and lower risk. The addition of bear-trap patterns as entry points adds another layer of reliability, allowing traders to enter positions with increased confidence, knowing that the market sentiment has decisively shifted in their favour. This approach not only improves entry timing but also enhances risk management, as the bear-trap provides a logical and strategic level for stop-loss placement.

Multi-year breakouts, while infrequent, offer long-term trend-following opportunities that align with broader market momentum and macroeconomic trends. Traders who master the art of identifying these setups on Point & Figure charts can potentially ride sustained trends, capturing gains that shorter-term strategies might miss. Moreover, applying fundamental filters, such as profitability metrics and growth indicators, can further enhance the effectiveness of these trades by ensuring that the stocks selected for multi-year breakouts are fundamentally strong, thereby reducing the risk of false breakouts.

Ultimately, the multi-year and multi-top breakout strategy is a testament to the power of patience, discipline, and technical insight. By blending classical chart patterns with modern tools and well-defined rules, traders can position themselves for substantial gains while effectively managing their risk. As with any trading strategy, consistency, and adherence to the process are crucial. With time, traders who practice and refine this approach can add a powerful, high-probability setup to their trading arsenal, capable of delivering impressive results in their trading journey.

Chapter 11

CRITICAL COMPONENT OF RISK MANAGEMENT

Every trader dreams of landing the perfect trade—those rare opportunities that can double, triple, or even more than multiply their capital. While it is exhilarating to think about those trades that deliver 5x, 10x, or even 20x returns, the fact remains that such opportunities are rare, and pursuing these big wins can be hazardous without proper risk management. Handling these trades recklessly can result in significant loss of capital.

This is where position sizing becomes crucial. By determining how much of your capital should be allocated to each trade, you are engaging in the bedrock of risk management. Position sizing ensures that you do not expose your portfolio to excessive risk in pursuit of massive gains. Instead, you can maximize your winners while minimizing the damage caused by your losers, helping you stay in the game for the long haul.

The goal of position sizing is to strike a balance between achieving significant returns and preserving your capital. When carried out correctly, it assures that your success is meaningful while safeguarding you from being ousted by any single failure in the market.

What is Position Sizing and why is it important?

In the grand scheme of trading, position sizing is not just another technique—it is a cornerstone of risk management that separates successful traders from those who succumb to emotional decision-making. It determines how much capital you allocate to a trade, allowing you to manage both the upside potential and the downside risk. By setting appropriate position sizes, traders protect themselves from overexposure to volatile markets and prevent the possibility of significant capital loss from just one bad trade.

Think of position sizing as your safety net. No matter how confident you are about a trade—whether you are using a Darvas Box setup, following a Turtle Trading trend, or a Multi-Timeframe P&F strategy—your risk should be carefully calibrated. Even the most promising trades can turn against you, but with well-calculated position sizing, a losing trade will not knock you out of the game.

For example, if you were trading a trend-following strategy like Turtle Trading, you might experience large price swings as part of the natural market cycle. In such cases, position sizing ensures that you are never risking too much of your portfolio on any one position. You can ride on market corrections, keeping your focus on the longer-term picture instead of worrying about short-term volatility wiping out your capital.

It is also about removing emotions from your trades. When you have predetermined your position size, you are less likely to be swayed by fear or greed. You can trade objectively, knowing that even if the market moves against you, you have already managed your risk. This objectivity is crucial in maintaining long-term consistency in the markets.

At the same time, you do not want to be too conservative. Position sizing is not just about limiting risk; it is about giving yourself enough room to capture upside potential. Too small of a position size can leave you missing out on significant returns. Too large of a position, and you risk emotional decisions or suffering steep losses.

In summary, position sizing is about finding the perfect balance—managing risk while allowing for substantial returns. It is the tool that helps traders navigate the uncertainties of the market and stay in the game for the long term. As you continue your trading journey, always remember that managing your position size is managing your future success.

In this chapter, I will use "portfolio" and "bets" interchangeably where appropriate.

Diversified vs. Concentrated Portfolios (Bets)

When considering position sizing, one of the key decisions you will have to take is whether to adopt a diversified or concentrated portfolio approach. Each has its merits and risks, and the choice between the two largely depends on your trading goals, risk tolerance, and personality.

A diversified portfolio is designed to spread risk across multiple stocks or assets. By allocating smaller positions across a broader range of securities, you reduce the impact that a single losing trade can have on your overall portfolio. This approach is often more stable and less volatile, acting as a cushion against unforeseen market downturns. However, while diversification helps manage risk, it can also limit the potential for large gains. Even if one stock in your portfolio performs exceptionally well, the impact on your total return will be muted due to the smaller position size.

On the other hand, a concentrated portfolio focuses on fewer stocks, with larger positions in each. This approach can lead to higher rewards if you choose the right stocks. A famous example of the success of a concentrated portfolio is Rakesh Jhunjhunwala's bet on Titan, a single stock that turned into a massive success and significantly boosted his wealth. However, the downside of concentration is clear—it is a high-risk strategy. If the stock does not perform as expected, the losses can be equally magnified, potentially damaging your portfolio.

While I lean towards a concentrated approach for wealth creation and trading, this strategy is not suited for everyone. It requires conviction, research, and the ability to tolerate higher volatility. For traders with lower risk tolerance, a diversified portfolio may be more appropriate, providing steady growth while protecting capital from large swings.

The choice between diversification and concentration is not a one-size-fits-all answer. It is about finding the balance that works for your individual strategy and goals. Whether you opt for a more diversified portfolio to manage risk or a concentrated one to seek larger gains, proper position sizing is crucial. It allows you to take advantage of market opportunities while ensuring that you are not overexposed to unnecessary risks. In the end, position sizing becomes the key to maximizing returns while safeguarding your capital.

How to Approach Position Sizing

Let us say you have Rs 10 lacs to invest in the stock market, and you have researched Company A, which is trading at Rs 1,000 per share. Should you buy 1,000 shares, or should you limit your exposure to 100 shares? If you commit all your capital to Company A, you are essentially betting the ranch—putting yourself at risk of losing a large chunk of your portfolio if the trade does not go your way.

Seth Klarman, a renowned investor, advises not to "bet the ranch on any single investment." Instead, he suggests a more nuanced approach where position sizing is determined based on conviction levels. If you strongly believe in a stock based on research and analysis, you may allocate a higher percentage of your capital. But if you are less certain, it makes sense to limit your exposure.

Klarman typically allocates positions as 3%, 5%, or 6% of his portfolio, depending on his conviction. However, he rarely goes above 10% unless there is a significant opportunity where he has a seat on the board or the company's intrinsic value can be unlocked. This approach allows him to balance between opportunities without overexposing his portfolio.

For traders using systems like Turtle Trading or any other system discussed in this book where trades often last for extended periods, a 1% or 2% exposure per trade can help protect against volatility. This approach ensures that no single loss will take a trader out of the game, while still allowing for significant upside if the trade works out.

Position Sizing Techniques

Let us explore some effective position-sizing techniques that can help you manage risk and optimize returns.

1. Fixed Dollar Value

This is the simplest approach, where you allocate a fixed amount of money to each trade. For example, if you have Rs 10 lacs, you might allocate Rs 1 lacs to each trade. This method is easy to implement but does not account for differences in the volatility or risk of each trade.

2. Fixed Percentage Risk Per Trade (Exposure Based)

In this method, you risk a fixed percentage of your capital on each trade. For example, if you are willing to risk 2% of Rs 10 lacs account on a single trade, you would risk Rs 20,000. This method is more flexible and takes into account the distance to your stop-loss, ensuring that you are not overexposed.

This technique is especially useful in trend-following strategies like Turtle Trading, Darvas Box, and Multi-timeframe P&F, or Dynamic Support where trades can involve significant price swings.

3. Volatility (ATR) Based

This technique involves using volatility indicators like Average True Range (ATR) to determine your position size. The more volatile the stock, the smaller your position should be to minimize risk. Conversely, less volatile stocks can be given larger positions.

This approach works well for Multi-Timeframe P&F trading, where different timeframes have varying volatility, requiring careful adjustment of position size. Even the Turtle Trading System considers volatility based stop-loss.

4. Kelly Criterion

The Kelly Criterion calculates the optimal position size based on the probability of winning trades and their potential returns. While this can maximize gains, it also involves larger-than-normal position sizes, which might not be suitable for everyone.

Traders with a Bollinger Band strategy, which focuses on identifying potential breakout stocks for short-term, may use the Kelly Criterion to size positions in high-probability trades, but should be cautious not to over-leverage.

Case Study

To better understand position sizing techniques, let us take a real-world example using the Turtle Trading system and walk through each position sizing technique with calculations. To make it more realistic, let us assume a starting capital of Rs 10 lacs, and we will focus on a trade in a trending stock that qualifies under our Turtle Trading strategy.

Let us assume we are considering a trade on ABC Ltd. using the Turtle Trading breakout system. The stock price has broken out above the 20-day high, signaling a long trade, and the stop-loss is placed at the 10-day low.

Here are some necessary inputs:

- Entry price of ABC Ltd.: Rs 500
- Stop-loss price: Rs 470
- Account size: Rs 10 lacs
- Risk tolerance per trade: 2%

1. Fixed Dollar Value

In this method, a trader allocates a fixed amount of capital to each trade. Let us assume we decide to allocate Rs 1 lakh to each trade from the total Rs 10 lacs.

- Trade allocation = Rs 1 lacs
- Entry price = Rs 500

To calculate the number of shares to buy, divide the allocated capital by the entry price:

$$Shares\,to\,buy = \frac{1,00,000}{500} = 200\,shares$$

In this method, we buy 200 shares of ABC Ltd. irrespective of the stop-loss distance or volatility. However, this method does not account for risk or stop-loss, which may cause inconsistent risk levels across different trades.

2. Fixed Percentage Risk Per Trade (Exposure Based)

In this method, we risk a fixed percentage of our total capital on each trade. Let us assume we are willing to risk 2% of Rs 10 lacs, which amounts to Rs 20,000.

Next, we calculate the risk per share, which is the difference between the entry price and the stop-loss price:

Risk per share = 500 -470 = Rs. 30

To calculate the number of shares to buy, divide the total risk tolerance (Rs 20,000) by the risk per share (Rs 30):

$$Shares\,to\,buy = \frac{20,000}{30} = 666\,shares$$

Here, we buy 666 shares of ABC Ltd. By using this method, we ensure that even if the trade hits the stop-loss, we will only lose 2% of our capital (Rs 20,000), allowing for consistent risk management.

This method is useful in trend-following strategies like Turtle Trading, where price swings can be significant. It ensures that, regardless of the volatility of each trade, your maximum risk remains controlled.

3. Volatility (ATR) Based Position Sizing

This method uses the Average True Range (ATR) to determine position size based on the stock's volatility. The higher the volatility (as measured by ATR), the smaller the position size, and vice versa.

Let us assume that ABC Ltd. has an ATR of 15. We are still willing to risk 2% of our capital (Rs 20,000) on this trade. First, calculate the ATR-based risk per share by multiplying the ATR by a factor (commonly 2):

ATR based risk per trade = ATR x 2 = 15 x 2 = Rs 30

Now, we calculate the number of shares to buy based on the total risk of Rs 20,000:

$$Shares\ to\ buy = \frac{20,000}{30} = 666\ shares$$

By adjusting the position size based on volatility, we reduce our exposure to highly volatile stocks, which minimizes the risk of being stopped out because of normal price fluctuations.

4. Kelly Criterion

The Kelly Criterion is a more advanced formula used to calculate the optimal position size based on the probability of winning and the expected return. It helps maximize gains but can involve larger position sizes, which might increase risk.

Let us assume that based on historical data, the probability of a successful trade in this system is 60%, and the reward-to-risk ratio is 3:1.

The Kelly Criterion formula is:

$$Kelly\ Percentage = P - \left(\frac{1-p}{R} \right)$$

Where:

- P = probability of success (0.60)
- R = reward-to-risk ratio (3)

$$Kelly\ Percentage = 0.60 - \left(\frac{1 - 0.60}{3} \right)$$

Kelly Percentage = 0.467

According to the Kelly Criterion, you would allocate 46.7% of your capital to this trade. However, such a large allocation could be too risky for most traders, so it is common to halve the Kelly percentage or even use 1/4th Kelly to stay conservative. Let us say we use 1/4th Kelly:

$$Adjusted\ Kelly\ Percentage = \frac{46.7\%}{4} = 11.675\%$$

This means we allocate 11.675% of our total capital of Rs 10 lakh to this trade:

Allocation = 11.675% x 10,00,000= Rs 1,16,750

With the entry price of Rs 500, we can buy:

$$Shares\ to\ buy = \frac{1,16,750}{500} = 233\ shares$$

The Kelly Criterion is more suited for traders who are highly confident in their system's edge and want to maximize returns. For example, in the Single Candle Breakout setup where high-probability breakout trades are the focus, the Kelly Criterion might encourage traders to size up on those with a proven statistical edge.

Position Sizing: Why You Need It

Position sizing helps protect your portfolio from being wiped out by short-term fluctuations while still giving you enough exposure to capture meaningful gains. According to James Dinan, an American investor, and hedge fund manager, the size of your position depends more on how much you can potentially lose rather than how much you can make.

As traders, we often focus on how much we can make from a successful trade, but it is equally important to consider how much you are prepared to lose if the market moves against you. Limiting your position size in high-risk trades allows you to stick around for the long term and continue finding opportunities.

The Key to Sustainable Trading Success

To wrap up, position sizing is a fundamental element of successful trading, often underappreciated by traders who fixate solely on finding the perfect entry and exit points. While technical analysis and strategies like Turtle Trading, Darvas Box, Multi-Timeframe P&F, or any method discussed in this book can identify excellent market opportunities, it is 'Position Sizing' that ultimately governs how effectively you manage risk and capitalize on those trades.

Whether you choose the Fixed Dollar Value approach for its simplicity, the Fixed Percentage Risk method for balanced exposure, the Volatility-Based (ATR) strategy for dynamic adjustments, or even the more aggressive Kelly Criterion, the objective remains the same: protecting your capital while maximizing potential returns. Each technique offers a unique framework for controlling risk on every trade, ensuring that you can navigate both winners and losers without jeopardizing your overall portfolio.

Position sizing is not just about handling individual trades—it is about building a sustainable, long-term trading career. By integrating the appropriate position-sizing techniques into your trading plan, you not only safeguard against catastrophic losses but also position yourself to take full advantage of the market's opportunities when they arise.

In the end, mastering position sizing is about balancing your emotions, tempering greed with caution, and ensuring you stay in the game long enough to enjoy the benefits of a well-crafted trading strategy. As you continue developing your own system, remember that successful trading hinges as much on risk management and position sizing as it does on identifying the next profitable trade.

Chapter 12

CRAFTING AN EFFICIENT STOCK BASKET

By the time you have reached this chapter, you have already learned about various classical trading strategies, including the details of my personal trading approach. Now, as we conclude this book, it's time to discuss a vital aspect of trading that helps bridge everything you have learned so far: stock selection. With around 3000 publicly traded securities in the Indian stock market alone, it is practically impossible to keep an eye on all of them. That is where the concept of crafting an efficient stock basket comes in, allowing traders to narrow their focus and capitalize on the best opportunities the market has to offer.

Stock selection is essential to efficient trading. It helps traders streamline their decision-making process, allowing them to manage their time and resources to focus better. Why is this important? Think of the stock market as a bustling marketplace full of different products. If you browse through every single option, you will lose time, energy, and focus. By creating a well-curated stock universe, you eliminate unnecessary distractions and zero in on the stocks that align with your trading strategy.

There are several ways to build this stock basket, each depending on the trader's style and objectives. One of the simplest approaches is to use pre-built baskets. These are essentially groups of stocks that have already been categorized for you, like the Nifty 50 or Nifty 100. These indexes include some of the biggest, most actively traded companies, offering a straightforward way to focus on established liquid stocks.

Sectoral baskets, like the banking or IT sector, also fall into this category and allow traders to target specific industries. For those interested in trading derivatives, you can focus on Futures and Options (F&O) stocks, which tend to be more actively traded.

A more personalized approach to building a stock universe involves using fundamental analysis. This method focuses on the financial health of companies and is ideal for traders and investors looking for strong long-term plays. Within this method, there are two main approaches. The absolute approach involves setting specific benchmarks, such as requiring a stock's Price-to-Earnings (P/E) ratio to be above a certain level or Return on Equity (ROE) to be above a fixed percentage. The relative approach compares a company's current financial performance to its past, looking for improvements in key metrics like ROE or Operating Profit Margins (OPM). With the help of stock screening tools, like the ones provided by platforms such as Radar by Definedge Securities, you can easily filter through companies based on these criterias, making it much easier to identify quality stocks.

Another popular method is the technical approach, where traders rely on price movements and chart patterns to pick stocks. Indicators like the Relative Strength Index (RSI), ADX (Average Directional Index), and MACD (Moving Average Convergence Divergence) can help you spot stocks with strong momentum. Chart patterns like cup-and-handle, triangle formations, or the head-and-shoulders pattern also serve as useful tools for identifying potential trading opportunities. The idea here is to rely on technical indicators and price action rather than financial fundamentals. This approach tends to work best for short-term and medium-term trading, where traders focus more on market trends than on a company's financial health.

One more unique approach is the idea of trading only one stock. While this might seem overly focused, there are benefits to it. By concentrating on a single stock, traders can develop an in-depth understanding of its price movements and behavior. Over time, this familiarity can lead to greater intuition about when to buy, sell, or hold. However, this strategy comes with its risks, mainly because you're putting all your eggs in one basket. With this approach, you lose out on diversification, and if the stock experiences a sudden downturn, it can significantly affect your portfolio.

In the end, the stock universe you build is a personal choice that reflects your strengths, goals, and trading style. Whether you choose to use pre-built baskets, fundamental filters, technical indicators, or focus solely on one stock, the key is to align your stock selection process with your strategy. By having a well-curated basket, you improve your chances of finding profitable trades, all while reducing the noise and distractions of the broader market.

The importance of crafting an efficient stock basket cannot be overstated. It streamlines your workflow, narrows your focus, and optimizes your chances for success. As you have learned throughout this book, trading is not just about mastering one strategy or one method. It is about building a comprehensive approach that integrates multiple techniques. Now, with a strong understanding of stock selection and technical strategies, you have all the tools needed to approach the market confidently. The next and final chapter will tie everything together, ensuring you have a complete toolkit to navigate the stock market with precision and purpose.

Chapter 13

TRADING PSYCHOLOGY - LESSONS FROM THE ICONS

Trading is a battlefield, but unlike traditional wars, the greatest enemy is often within. It is a journey where the mind, not just the market, dictates success or failure. Trading psychology is not as quantifiable as technical indicators, and it does not fit neatly into chart patterns like a Darvas Box or Triangle Pattern. Yet, it is the single most important factor that separates successful traders from those who merely survive—or worse, lose consistently. Teaching and learning trading psychology is not straightforward. The lessons are often subtle, internal, and deeply personal. But psychology is the invisible glue that binds everything together, whether you are executing a multi-timeframe P&F setup or riding a trend with Turtle Trading rules. Through the stories of real-life icons, whose mastery extends far beyond financial markets, we will uncover critical psychological traits that traders need to cultivate for long-term success.

One of the greatest cricketers in history, Mahendra Singh Dhoni, is known not only for his performance but also for his incredible ability to stay calm under pressure. Imagine the tense moments in the final overs of a cricket match—the stakes are high, the fans are roaring, and a single mistake could cost the game. In these scenarios, Dhoni remains unflustered, a trait that traders need to emulate when navigating volatile markets. During an interview, Dhoni was asked, "How do you manage to stay so calm under pressure?" His reply was simple but profound: "I don't think about the result; it is the result that creates pressure. I focus on what I can control—improving my technique, reading the situation, and making the best possible decisions based on the current conditions." This mindset is essential in trading, especially when executing strategies like Darvas Box or Turtle Trading. Traders often fixate on the outcome of a trade—how much they will make or lose—and this fixation on results can paralyze decision-making. You might have a perfect Darvas Box breakout setup, but if you are consumed by the potential result, fear might cause you to exit prematurely, or greed might make you hold on too long, deviating from the strategy. Like Dhoni, successful traders understand that the outcome of a single trade is irrelevant; it is the long-term process that matters. You cannot control the market any more than Dhoni can control the pitch, but you can control your approach—whether it is sticking to your rules in a Turtle Trading system or ensuring your stop-loss is properly set in a P&F trade. The key is to remain calm, focus on the process, and not let the outcome of individual trades dictate your emotions.

Late Lata Mangeshkar is revered for her impeccable precision in singing. Whether performing a slow ballad or a high-energy track, every note she hit was perfect, every word pronounced with clarity. This level of mastery did not come from raw talent alone; it was honed through years of practice, discipline, and an obsessive attention to detail. Shreya Ghoshal, herself a celebrated singer, once remarked on Lata ji's attention to detail, especially in "antra" (the precise pronunciation of every syllable). Even after achieving legendary status, Lata ji never let herself falter in this regard, treating every performance as an opportunity to maintain her high standards. In trading, it is not just about identifying a setup; it is about executing it flawlessly, without hesitation, without cutting corners. For instance, a trader using the Multi-timeframe Point & Figure (P&F) strategy might see a buy signal on a 1% P&F chart, confirmed by a breakout on the 3% chart. If, at the moment of execution, you hesitate or second-guess the signal, you risk missing out on the opportunity. Just like Lata ji's precision in hitting every note, a trader must execute every trade with precision, trusting their setup and rules.

Sachin Tendulkar, widely regarded as one of the greatest cricketers of all time, embodies the importance of adaptability and mastery. A famous story shared by cricket commentator Harsha Bhogle illustrates this perfectly. Tendulkar was playing with a bat that was heavily taped, similar to how children might patch up their favourite bat when they can not afford a new one. Despite this, Tendulkar was performing at the highest level. One day, however, he came onto the field with a brand-new bat. When asked why he switched, he explained that during the last game, he played a cover drive that did not travel as it should have, so he knew it was time for a change. Tendulkar did not wait for a full-blown failure to change his bat; he adjusted at the first sign of a minor issue. This anecdote offers a profound lesson for traders: knowing when to adapt and make adjustments is crucial. If your trade setup is not behaving as expected, it might be time to reassess your position or strategy, even if the market has not fully turned against you yet. Tendulkar's mastery came from knowing his craft so intimately that he could sense subtle changes in performance. As traders, developing a similar mastery allows us to recognize when a trend is weakening, when volatility is increasing, or when the fundamentals of a stock are shifting.

Bollywood superstar Shah Rukh Khan might seem like an unusual role model for traders, but his career offers profound insights into the importance of mindset and resilience. SRK, as he is fondly known, did not come from a film family and entered Bollywood with no connections and no backing. Yet, through sheer determination, he rose to become one of the most successful actors in the world. SRK's story is about daring to be different. Early in his career, he took on negative roles that many actors would not have dared to touch. This bold move could have easily backfired, but it paid off, setting him apart from his peers. Similarly, in trading, the market rewards those who are willing to think independently, those who are not afraid to step outside the crowd and try a different strategy. Whether it is adapting a new technical setup or riding a trend when others are fearful, having the courage to walk your own path is often the difference between success and mediocrity. SRK also openly discusses the importance of resilience. In an interview, he once said, "Success is not a good teacher; failure makes you humble." Every trader will experience failure, whether it is a losing trade, a strategy that stops working, or a market that suddenly turns. The key is not avoiding failure—it is learning from it. A losing Darvas Box setup does not mean the strategy is broken; it just means that particular trade did not work out. Resilience means sticking to your plan, learning from your mistakes, and moving forward with confidence.

Each of these stories—Dhoni's calmness, Lata ji's precision, Tendulkar's adaptability, and SRK's resilience—directly connects to the trading strategies we have discussed throughout this book. In Darvas Box trading, for instance, calmness is required to patiently wait for the box breakout, while precision is needed to enter and exit at the right levels. The Turtle Trading strategy demands adaptability as market trends shift, and resilience is key when riding out long trends in volatile markets. The same holds true for the Single Candle Breakout strategy, where attention to detail is critical. You need the mental discipline to trust your setup and not let the noise of the market throw you off your game. Whether you are waiting for a confirmation on the larger timeframe or managing a trade on the shorter timeframe, the mental game is what keeps you aligned with your strategy.

As you progress further on your trading journey, remember that success is not just about perfecting technical strategies. It is about mastering the mental game. Trading is an intensely personal journey where the greatest battles are often fought within. Your mindset, your ability to remain calm under pressure, your discipline, and your resilience are the keys to long-term success. Just as Dhoni remains unfazed under pressure, Lata ji's strives for perfection, Tendulkar adapts at the right moment, and Shah Rukh Khan perseveres against all odds, you must cultivate these same qualities in your trading. Master the psychology of trading, and the strategies you have learned will become far more powerful tools in your hands. Your journey is not just about learning to trade; it is about becoming a master of yourself. In trading, that is what truly separates those who succeed from those who do not.

CONCLUSION

• •

As we come to the end of this learning journey, it is essential to reflect on everything we have covered and revisit the principles that will help you build a resilient foundation in trading and investing. This book was crafted with a singular aim: to equip you with the knowledge, tools, and mindset needed to navigate financial markets confidently and effectively. Each chapter, every case study, and each concept is part of a larger mosaic designed to guide you towards success. As you move forward, keep in mind that trading is not just about acquiring techniques but about developing a disciplined approach to the markets.

We began with the building blocks of a strong foundation, focusing on the core principles of trading and investing. Understanding Trend, Relative Strength, Fundamental Analysis, embracing discipline, and adhering to a well-thought-out strategy set the stage for a systematic approach to trading. These foundational concepts were introduced as the essential groundwork; they are not something you outgrow as you become more advanced. Instead, these basics remain the bedrock of all sophisticated trading strategies, providing stability even as the markets shift and evolve. Never underestimate the power of returning to these fundamental truths when faced with complexity.

Mastering technical analysis and understanding price patterns are pivotal elements of our exploration. Through Triangle, Rectangle, and Cup & Handle formations, you learned to interpret price movements and understand the psychology driving these patterns. Recognizing these setups and understanding their formation provides you with an edge, helping you anticipate potential price movements with greater accuracy. Each pattern serves as a critical insight into the market's current state, and combining them with the right setups, like buildup or breakout, can increase confidence in your trades. These patterns are essentially the market's language, and learning to "speak" this language brings clarity to what might otherwise seem chaotic.

Beyond reading charts, we explored the power of position sizing and risk management. If technical analysis is the art of spotting trends, then position sizing and risk management are the sciences of staying in the game. Through techniques like calculating optimal position sizes, setting strategic stop-losses, and employing trailing stop-losses, we delved into methods for safeguarding your capital. The reality of trading is that no strategy can guarantee success every time, and even the most carefully planned trades can incur losses. Position sizing allows you to participate in multiple trades without risking your capital on any single position, and robust risk management ensures that no single trade has the potential to derail your journey. These principles form your safety net, helping you endure downturns and come back with renewed focus.

As we delved into trend-following systems and classical strategies like Darvas Box, Turtle Trading, and Multi-Timeframe Point & Figure, we discovered powerful frameworks for capturing large market moves. These strategies are designed for traders who are willing to commit to the discipline and patience required to ride trends. Each strategy introduced is a complete system with clear entry, exit, and risk management rules, enabling you to create a robust framework aligned with your personal trading objectives. By staying committed to these principles, you are not just following trends but also developing the mental resilience needed to avoid emotional decisions.

Consolidation and buildup patterns hold a special place in technical analysis, as they signify equilibrium before the next significant move. These are the moments when the market pauses, reflecting a balance between buyers and sellers. Recognizing these patterns can provide an advantage by positioning you to capture explosive moves when the market eventually breaks out. Consolidation is a reminder of the importance of patience in trading, underscoring that sometimes the best trades come to those who wait. These buildup patterns often give rise to high-probability setups that traders can leverage for effective entries and exits, allowing for precision and reduced risk.

We also examined the importance of trailing stop-loss methods, exploring techniques that allow you to stay in winning trades longer and capture extended moves. Whether using moving averages, SuperTrend, or the three-candle rule, trailing stop-losses offer flexibility in capturing maximum gains while managing downside risk. This flexibility can be especially valuable in strong, trending markets, where maximizing the trend's full potential can make a significant difference in overall profitability. In essence, trailing stop-losses help you balance your need for security with the desire to capture ongoing momentum.

No journey in trading is complete without addressing trading psychology, as markets are driven by emotion as much as they are by logic. Developing the right trading psychology is about cultivating patience, resilience, and self-control. It is about adhering to your trading plan, managing losses without discouragement, and maintaining a level-headed approach amid market volatility. We took inspiration from high achievers like Mahendra Singh Dhoni, Lata Mangeshkar, and Sachin Tendulkar, and SRK, whose discipline and dedication parallel what it takes to succeed in trading. Just like them, the mental toughness you build as a trader will set you apart in a landscape that often tests emotional endurance as much as skill.

Trading is not a get-rich-quick endeavor but a journey of ongoing learning, discipline, and personal growth. Every trade you place is a new opportunity to refine your strategy, improve your execution, and learn from the outcomes. Success in trading comes from consistent, methodical execution of your plan, steadfast adherence to risk management, and a commitment to continual self-improvement. Mistakes and losses are inevitable; approach them as learning experiences that contribute to your development. Trading is as much about managing your internal landscape—your emotions, discipline, and resilience—as it is about external market factors.

This book is designed to be a reference you can revisit whenever you need guidance or a refresher on critical concepts. Markets evolve, strategies shift, and you, as a trader, will grow and adapt along with them. Keep honing your skills, stay disciplined, and maintain confidence in the process you have developed. May this book serve as a trusted companion on your trading journey, offering clarity and direction when markets become uncertain.

I wish you all the success and prosperity that diligent, thoughtful, and disciplined trading can bring. Remember, every successful trader once started as a beginner. With persistence, patience, and an unwavering commitment to your journey, you too can achieve your financial goals. Good luck, and may your trading journey be both fulfilling and rewarding.

Kaushik Akiwatkar

BIBLIOGRAPHY

Aby, Carroll D. J. Point & Figure Charting: The Complete Guide. Grinville, SC: Traders Press Inc., 1996.

Bollinger, John. Bollinger on Bollinger Bands, New York, NY: McGraw-Hill, 2002. Bulkowski, Thomas N. Encyclopaedia of Chart Patterns. New York, NY: John Wiley & Sos, Inc., 2000.

Carney, Scott M. Harmonic Trading, Volume One: Profiting from the Natural Order of the Financial Markets. FT Press; 1 edition (April 22, 2010)

Covel, Michael W. The Complete TurtleTrader. HarperCollins e-books (2009).

Dorsey, Thomas J. Point & Figure charting: The Essential Applications for Forecasting and Tracking Market Prices. Hoboken, New Jersey: John Wiley & Sons, Inc., 2007

Douglas, Mark. Trading in the Zone. Prentice-Hall Press, 2001.

Du Plessis, Jeremy, The Definitive Guide to Point and Figure: A comprehensive Guide to the Theory and Practical Use of the Point and Figure Charting Method, Petersfield: Harriman House Publishing, 2006.

Edwards, R., and J. Magee. Technical Analysis of Stock Trends, 8th ed., 2003. 1948 edition revised by W. H. C. Bassetti, St. Lucie Press, Boca Raton, FL.

Elder, Alexander. Trading for Living. New York, NY: John Wiley & Sons, Inc., 1993.

Faith, Curtis. Way of the Turtle: The Secret Methods that Turned Ordinary People into Legendary Traders. McGraw-Hill Education, 2007.

Kaufman, Perry J. Trading Systems and Methods, 3rd ed. New York, NY: John Wiley & Sons, Inc., 1998.

Kirkpatrick, Charles D., and Dahlquist, Julie R. The Complete Resource for Financial Market Technicians. New Jersey: Pearson Education, Inc., 2007

Minervini, Mark. Trade Like a Stock Market Wizard: How to Achieve Super Performance in Stocks in Any Market. McGraw-Hill Education, 2013.

Minervini, Mark. Think & Trade Like a Champion: The Secrets, Rules & Blunt Truths of a Stock Market Wizard, Access Publishing Group, LLC (2017).

Morris, George, L. The Complete Guide to Market Breadth Indicators: How to Analyze and Evaluate Market Direction and Strength, Gregory L. Morris; Second Edition (2015).

Murphy, John J., Intermarket Analysis, New Jersey: John Wiley & Sons, Inc., 2004.

Nison, Steve, Japanese Candlestick Charting Techniques, New York, NY: New York Institute of Finance, 2001.

O'Neil, William J.; O'Neil, William J. How to Make Money in Stocks: A Winning System in Good Times and Bad, Fourth Edition. McGraw-Hill Education, 4th Edition, 2009.

Pring, Martin J., Technical Analysis Explained: The Successful Investor's Guide to Spotting Investment Trends and Turning Points, McGraw-Hill, 2002.

Schwager, Jack D. Market Wizards. New York, NY: New York Institute of Finance, 1989.

Taleb, Nassim. Fooled by Randomness. Penguin, 2007.

Tharp, Van K. Trade Your Way to Financial Freedom. McGraw-Hill Education; 2nd edition., 2006.

Tharp, Van K. Definitive Guide to Position Sizing Strategies. The Van Tharp Institute, 2nd edition, 2013.

Wheelan, Alexander, Study Helps in Point and Figure Technique, Morgan Rogers and Roberts, New York, 1954 and Traders Press, Greenville, 1990.

Wilder, J. Welles Jr. New Concepts in Technical Trading Systems. Greensboro, SC: Trend Research, 1978.

Zieg, Kermit C., Point & Figure Commodity & Stock Trading Techniques, Traders Press, Greenville, 1997.

Prashant Shah, Trading the Markets the Point & Figure Way, Notion Press, 1st Edition, Chennai, 2018

Prashant Shah, Profitable Trading with Renko Charts, Vision Books, 1st Edition, Delhi, 2019

Prashant Shah, Outperforming the Markets using Relative Strength And Breadth analysis, 1st Edition, Notion Press, Chennai, 2021